MUSICAL STAGES

To Dorothy
with thanks and love

I am indebted to Stanley Green
and Rita M. Chambers for their
help in researching material
for this book.

Richard Rodgers

MUSICAL STAGES

They carried my great-grandmother's coffin down in one of those elevators that started and stopped when the elevator man tugged at a steel cable running through the car. The coffin was a plain pine box and had lain on a bed of ice on the floor for only a few hours before it was taken away. The ice took the place of embalming, strictly forbidden, and the body had to be removed almost immediately. This hurried ritual was the end of orthodox Judaism in our family. The next step was known as Reform, and even this faded after the bar mitzvah of my brother and me as a gesture to my grandfather on my mother's side. From that time on, my parents, my brother and I were Jewish for socioethnic reasons rather than because of any deep religious conviction.

If you walked south from my great-grandmother's house on Fifth Avenue down to 124th Street and turned west to Mt. Morris Park West, then walked south again to 120th Street, you would find yourself at the southwest corner of Mt. Morris Park, one of the prettiest little parks in New York. One house to the west, 3 West 120th Street, was home. Down a few steps was what was known and pronounced as an "airy-way." An iron-grill door led into the service entrance, and past two servants' rooms to the kitchen. Back of this was a pantry with a dumbwaiter serving the dining room, two floors above.

3 West 120th Street was a brownstone-stoop house. In wintertime, rubber steps and a wooden balustrade had to be put down because the stone was murderously slippery and my father's medical practice was not so small that he needed accidents at the front door. Inside was what everyone called the vestibule. A second door led into my father's province. Here we had to be very quiet because there might be a patient waiting in the reception room. Farther down the hall was the office, and beyond that a mysterious place known as the examining room, where occasionally I was allowed to watch my father pour an amber fluid into a glass tube, light a small flame under it, dip a piece of thin paper in the fluid and make a pronouncement concerning the patient. In those days the family doctor did the urinalysis himself without the luxury of an expensive laboratory.

One flight up began the living quarters for the family, which consisted of my mother's parents, my grandmother's bachelor brother, my parents, my brother and me. There was a dining room and a pantry, the terminus for the dumbwaiter. Then, facing 120th Street, came the living room. And what a room it was to me! There was a carved oak table in the center of the floor, a huge sofa and comfortable chairs covered with some kind of green material. But the main object in the room—indeed in the house, indeed in my life—was the Steinway upright near the window. It had green cloth on either side of the music rack and there was a green piano stool with green tassels. When I was little more than a baby I used to love to make the seat spin and watch the tassels fly out. It was then that I learned that exciting sounds came from the piano itself when my mother played it. This was the beginning of my lifelong love affair with music.

My passion for music was not accidental. The piano was the one means through which I could escape from the generally unpleasant atmosphere of my family life. There was hostility between my father and his mother-in-law, between my grandmother and grandfather, and between my brother and me. To find some of the reasons that produced these strained relationships, it's important to know something about the backgrounds of the people who made up our family.

My mother's father, Jacob Levy, who had come to this country with very little money, went into the silk business and ended up a rich man. He married Rachel Lewine in 1869, and Mamie, my mother, was the second of their three children. My father's parents had come from Russia by way of France and had settled briefly in a small town in Missouri named Holden. (Why Holden, I haven't the slightest idea.) William, my father, was born there but within a year his family had moved to New York. Originally the family name was rather long, but somewhere in it was a sound that approximated "Rodgers." I think that for a time the name Abrams was used, and I've been told that at least one member of my father's family used a variation of Abrams which came out Brahms. All I'm sure of is that when my father graduated from college his name was Rodgers.

William Rodgers—he was never called anything but Will—was the oldest of eight children. His father had died before I was born and his mother soon after, but I do remember my father's grandmother quite vividly—particularly her funeral and that plain pine coffin. There was little money in the Rodgers family, and as a young man Pop had to earn a living as a customs officer on the docks while simultaneously studying to be a doctor. He had been practicing medicine for about three years when he met, fell in love with and married my mother.

It was at this point that my folks made a serious mistake. My mother's parents did not want their only daughter to leave them even after her marriage. And she, being a shy, insecure woman, had neither the desire nor the strength to break the ties. So, grudgingly, my father and mother moved in with Mom's parents. This, of course, turned out to be no solution at all, and was the chief cause for the hostile atmosphere that pervaded our home.

The antagonism between my father and his mother-in-law was understandable. Both were stubborn and opinionated, but their clashes stemmed primarily from my father's financial dependence—at least initially—on the Levys, and also from his unhappiness at his mother-in-law's domination of his wife. The disaffection between the two was shown not alone with words, but most often with silence. Frequently weeks went by without either speaking to the other, a situation that left me with a deep feeling of tension and insecurity.

Almost everything in our ménage at 3 West 120th Street contradicted almost everything else. My grandfather yelled a lot, but he had a great reservoir of love for the whole family. I remember occasionally entering his room and asking for the evening paper. His answer was always prefaced by the run-together word "Goddamittohell!" Then: "Get out of here!" I would go to my room and wait. Within minutes he would appear at my door, hand me the evening paper and pat me on the cheek. I loved him dearly. He was a very short man of normal weight but extremely impressive because of his habits of dress and deportment. From his carefully trimmed Vandyke beard to his highly polished shoes he looked exactly what he was: the patriarch of the family.

I lived under the same roof with this diminutive, domineering, untutored man until I was in my twenties. To this day my wife, who never met him, cannot understand why we all loved him, with his rough voice and his demanding nature and his unwillingness to compromise. Still, there was something irresistible about a little man who wore a square bowler, dressed impeccably, and would not wait for traffic to stop when he crossed the street. My mother would say, "Poppa, you'll get hurt if you don't watch the cars." His answer was always the same: "Let them watch me!" There was also something endearing to me about a man who did not speak very much to a small boy but who would never pass the chair he was sitting in without patting him gently on the cheek.

Another contradiction in the Levy-Rodgers household was that my father and his father-in-law got along so well. Logically, it should have been otherwise. It was Grandpa who had the money while Pop was struggling to build his practice. But these two strong-willed, strong-voiced men, both disciplinarians with fiery tempers, had a beautiful relationship until the day my grandfather died. That was in 1928, and it was Pop who stayed with him at his bedside to the very end, holding his hand.

Grandma was also full of contradictions. Though born in Europe, she had few ties to the Old Country. She had obvious disdain for her husband because, among other things, he had never lost his Russian accent, whereas her English was perfect. She was an avowed atheist and even made fun of Grandpa's religious beliefs. She was such an omniverous reader that whenever anyone in the family wanted to know the meaning of a word, he never had to consult the dictionary. "Don't bother looking it up, ask Grandma," was an expression heard frequently in our house. She was a know-it-all, and I suppose this rankled my father as much as anything else about her.

My grandmother's bachelor brother, Uncle Sam, also lived with us, though most of the time we were told that he was away at his "club," whatever that was. He was a strapping, handsome man, good-natured, affectionate and full of jokes. As far as my brother and I were concerned, he added a touch of glamour to our quarrelsome household.

I suppose it's only natural, but when I was a kid I thought my father was a tall man. Actually, he was of medium height, though his military bearing did give him the appearance of being a good deal taller. He had strong, even features, and I particularly remember his bright-red hair. Like Grandpa, he too had a Vandyke beard, though he later shaved it off.

Pop played a greater part in my life than anyone else. I must have been only an infant at the time, but I can recall clearly the way he used to toss me in the air and the feeling of warm security in being caught by his strong, gentle arms. But he did have a temper. Though his anger was rarely turned on me, the strength of his voice frightened me so that even today a loud voice makes me uncomfortable.

My mother liked to recall that when I was a child I once said to her, "You're the smallest mother in the world." Perhaps she wasn't *that* small, but tiny she was, and round. Not fat, really, just round. Her voice, too, was round and deep, and her round hands were comforting on those rare occasions when she would take one of mine in hers at the dining-room table and squeeze it gently. This sort of display of affection did not come easily to her, which made it all the dearer to me. I also remember the times when I went to bed with a bad cold and awoke in the middle of the night to the sound of slippered feet padding across my bedroom floor, feel the back of that round hand on my forehead and hear a whispered "Normal. Go back to sleep." Then a light kiss and the retreating sound of slippered feet.

My brother, Mortimer (Morty, Mort), and I had a relationship that I'm sure confirms all of today's fancy psychological words and phrases. As siblings, we were ambivalent toward each other, with strong love-hate feelings for which neither of us could be blamed. I feared him because he was four and a half years older than I, much stronger, and didn't hesitate to use his strength on me. I do recall, however, one time when a bigger boy attacked me in the street and Morty miraculously appeared and sent the fellow flying. But there was reason enough for him to feel that so far as the family was concerned, I was his enemy. In those early days he was known around the house as "the big one" and I was "the little feller." Since it was "the little feller" who followed Mom onto the piano stool and got a lot of attention, "the big one" was left frustrated and belligerent.

I am sure our career decisions were greatly influenced by this. If I could do what Mom did, it was only natural for Morty to want to do what Pop did. If I got recognition in the family with music, he'd get it with medicine. And eventually he did—not only within the family, but from his colleagues and patients as well.

Taken individually, the people who made up the Rodgers-Levy household—even Grandma—were not hard for me to get along with. But mealtime, when the antagonists were all together, was sheer hell. Bickering, yelling or unnatural silence were the norm, often with one family member storming upstairs before dinner was over.

Nor was the atmosphere around the dinner table helped by any culinary imagination. Each day in the week had its own main course that was served only on that day. Monday was pot roast, Tuesday was chicken, Wednesday was fish, and so on. This never varied. The only bright spot of the week was Sunday-night supper, when we would be treated to cold cuts from Pomerantz's Delicatessen.

In a house so full of friction and tensions it was important to me to find one place where I could enjoy some measure of peace and happiness, and this was the corner of the living room with the lovely piano, which my mother played so beautifully while she and my father sang. And what did they play and sing? Songs from the current musical shows on Broadway. Both my parents were avid theatregoers, with a special passion for musicals, and since the complete vocal-piano score was always sold in the theatre lobby, Pop never failed to buy a copy. So home would come *Mme. Modiste, The Merry Widow, The Chocolate Soldier* and all the rest to go up on the piano rack. They would be played so often, both before and after dinner, that I soon knew all the songs by heart.

These were the happy moments in not very happy days. There were no loud-voiced arguments then; voices were raised only in song. And in the middle of the fun stood little Richard, who received nothing but praise and love because his ear was so quick and he sang so well. Then when company came I was called on to perform, using the hearth near the piano as a stage. More praise and more love! Is it any wonder that I turned to music as a career, and that I made theatre music my particular field? Or that sixty-odd years later I am still enchanted by it?

I don't know exactly how old I was when I first tried to play the piano, but I gather that I had to be lifted onto the piano stool. I had heard all those beautiful sounds my mother could make simply by pressing her fingers down on the keys, and I wanted more than anything else to be able to make the same beautiful sounds. I wasn't much more than a toddler when I discovered that I was able to reproduce the melodies with accuracy.

When I was about six, a girl named Constance Hyman, the daughter of a college friend of my father's, taught me to play "Chopsticks." From then on I could manipulate the bass of "Chopsticks" with my left hand so that it would fit the melody of any song I was trying to reproduce with my right hand. Formal piano lessons, however, were not successful, chiefly because being able to play by ear made me lazy and I never bothered to practice. Why waste time reading notes when I could play just about anything I heard simply by listening?

Time after time I am asked if this gift for music was inherited or if it came as the result of being surrounded by musical sounds at an early age under the happiest possible circumstances. It's the old question: Are these drives genetic or environmental? The psychologists I have talked to cannot give a clear answer, and neither can I. In my case, both motivations are possible: a mother who was an accomplished musician and parents who provided me with the joys of music at a time when I desperately needed something in my life that would give me pleasure. I quickly discovered, too, that my parents' response to my love of music was their love of me, and family friends thought I was darling. Why wouldn't I rise to all this delicious bait? Although my brother was several years older and physically many times stronger, I could beat hell out of him merely by stepping to the piano. If theatre music could win me such affection and praise, as well as making me feel like the strongest kid on the block, then that was the kind of music for me.

Naturally, no two composers for the musical theatre have the identical background and environment, nor does there seem to be any consistency in the factors that shaped their interest and talent. In the case of George Gershwin, there was no musical leaning shown by either his mother or father; of the previous generation, one of his grandfathers was an Army engineer, the other a furrier.

Jerome Kern is a little easier. His father planned a business career for him, but his mother encouraged his musical interest and was accomplished enough to give him piano lessons when he was five years old.

Cole Porter's grandfather, a tough timber-and-mining baron, wanted Cole to be a lawyer. His mother, however, was more concerned about his being accepted in society. Thinking that music would help in that direction, she made sure that he was given piano lessons when he was a child. Cole wrote his first song at the age of ten, and from then on he never stopped satisfying his mother's ambition.

Another composer-lyricist, Harold Rome, was influenced by a mother who loved to sing and an uncle who played the violin. Like Cole Porter, he first studied law; unlike Porter, he also studied architecture and art before eventually succumbing to music.

A study of Frank Loesser's life reveals little that solves the environment-genetics puzzle. Both his parents were intellectual and his father taught music, but Frank refused to take piano lessons. Even though he began improvising tunes at the age of six, most of his early career was spent as a lyricist. On the other hand, both Frederick Loewe and Jule Styne were piano prodigies who were performing with symphony orchestras even before their teens.

Vincent Youmans, Sr., a wealthy hatter, had a Wall Street career planned for his son. Although Vincent, Jr., received musical encouragement from his mother, he did not begin to compose until he entered the Navy in World War I. No one seems to know where the impulse came from, but there can be no doubt about the strength of the drive and the extent of the talent.

Arthur Schwartz lived with a father who was strongly against music and a mother who loved it. She even had him take piano lessons in secret, for which he was punished. Did Arthur lean toward music because he resented his father or because he loved his mother?

Little is known about Irving Berlin beyond the fact that his father was born in Russia and was a cantor, hardly enough to account for one of the greatest songwriting talents the world has ever known. Both Harold Arlen's and Kurt Weill's fathers were also cantors. Noël Coward's father was not, but that did not seem to hurt his career.

It is obvious from these brief observations that no definite conclusions regarding the importance of background or surroundings can be drawn, other than that the influence of either or both cannot be denied. However, it is fair to say that mothers showed greater sympathy than fathers when their sons voiced ambitions to pursue musical careers. In this respect I was especially lucky, perhaps even unique; both my parents never expressed anything but total support and encouragement.

Besides the piano in the living room, the one place I loved in my neighborhood was Mt. Morris Park. Since it was just across the street, I would often go there to coast down the hill on a sled in winter and climb the hill to the bell tower in spring and fall. This tower had been put up originally as a lookout for fires, but I don't recall its ever having been used. The view from the top is still a fine one. I also recall that every spring the Parks Department would plant masses of tulips in the center of a little island at the intersection of 120th Street and Mt. Morris Park West.

The family schedule then was to move to Long Island in May (first Arverne, later Long Beach), where my father had his "summer practice," and back to 120th Street in September for his "winter practice." The summer patients paid better because there were lots of cuts to sew up and broken bones to set on a one-time basis, whereas the winter patients, who were mostly regular, enjoyed a somewhat lower rate.

The Benjamin Feiners and my parents were old friends. They spent the summer of 1909 near us at Arverne while their son, Benjy, aged five, was recuperating from typhoid under the care of my father. When Ben was well enough to sit on the porch I was taken one afternoon to play with him. Although I was only seven I remember the occasion well for two reasons: first, Ben's head had been shaved bald; secondly, he had a brand-new baby sister, two months old. Her nurse wheeled her out on the porch, and for the first time I looked upon my future and present wife.

Returning to New York was always exciting. There were usually enough kids on the block for a game of stickball, or if no other boys were around, there was always stoop ball, in which we would throw a golf ball from the edge of the gutter against a stoop and try to catch it for a score of one. It counted ten if we caught it after it hit the leading edge of the step. Invariably, late in the afternoon a window would go up and we would hear an elderly mother—usually someone in her early thirties—cry out, "Jimmy, come in and get washed for supper!" Getting washed for supper was mandatory, since the other untidy users of the street were the horses that drew the carriages and wagons which were still the major means of transportation.

We had a subway at 116th Street and the trolleys on Lenox Avenue, but the first automobile on our street was a major event. It belonged to a Dr. Hyman, who lived just across the street from us. This imposing machine was a green Maxwell and made the doctor's son, Arthur, the envy of the neighborhood. Arthur and I were good friends, but I never got a ride in the glorious Maxwell. Not long afterward my father got his own auto, a blue two-seater Mitchell, in which he used to pay calls in Arverne. I was often allowed to ride with him; it meant company for him and excitement for me. Naturally, I was never permitted in the patient's house, but it was fun to watch my father find a ledge on which to leave his cigar while he went indoors, and I enjoyed looking at the street from the vantage point of the high, ungainly Mitchell. Occasionally there would be an emergency call and I never could understand why Pop drove so slowly. One day he explained to me, "No doctor ever saved a life by getting there half a minute sooner." Many years later, when I had a severe heart attack, I realized how wrong he could be.

The Model School, between Seventh Avenue and St. Nicholas Avenue on 119th Street, was a training institution for public-school teachers, and there I learned the rudiments of English grammar and arithmetic. Intellectually, there is nothing to remember; socially, there was one fistfight with a tough kid who beat me up. I went home with a black eye and a bloody nose, but instead of the scolding I had expected, my father cleaned me up and said, "The important thing is—what did you do to the other guy?" My mother laughed, and once again I found my family in my corner.

Because my grandfather used to be away all day at some mysterious place called "the office" in some mysterious location called "downtown," our house was left in my father's charge. His domain was the second floor, the center of which was his consulting room. It was there that my parents may have made their first mistake with me. As I was leaving for school one morning, my mother told me I was to come home at lunchtime and not loiter on the way; she was going to have a surprise for me.

All morning at school I kept thinking about that surprise. Could it be the circus? Or a baseball game? Maybe I was even going to be taken to one of those musical shows my parents loved so much. But no matter what the treat would be, I knew I would enjoy it twice as much because it meant having a half-day off from school.

As soon as the midday bell rang, I dashed home as quickly as possible. Ma was waiting for me at the door, a tense smile on her rather pale face. The surprise turned out to be the news that my adenoids were to be operated on. Right then. Before lunch? No lunch. But I wasn't to worry. It wouldn't hurt because I'd be asleep and there was a pretty trained nurse to take care of me. I was led into Pop's big consulting room. My fear and disappointment were compounded when I saw the nurse. She wasn't pretty at all; she was unattractive and I resented it.

In those days, hospitals were used only for vital illnesses and really serious surgery, so Pop's familiar office had been transformed into a complete operating room. An operating table had been moved in, along with a row of gleaming instruments, and there was a strange man (the surgeon, I supposed) as well as the nurse. After I was undressed and on the table, a mask was put over my face. I heard a terrible roaring in my ears, and the next thing I knew I was lying on my mother's bed, my throat aching. I wanted desperately to have a drink of water, but I was too busy vomiting. The whole family was sweet and kind to me, but I couldn't get over the feeling that I had been tricked.

As the Model School taught children only through the second year, I was soon shipped off to P.S. 10 at 117th Street and St. Nicholas Avenue. This was big-time stuff; it was my brother's school! It was also Bennett Cerf's and Ben Grauer's, but we didn't get to know one another until years later.

Going to school was of little significance to me. I was never a good student; I got passing grades because I was moderately bright, and in general the teachers liked me. Much more important to me was my first brush with the theatre. Only five blocks away, on 125th Street, DeWolf Hopper was appearing in *The Pied Piper.* I was taken to a Saturday matinée, by whom I don't recall, nor do I remember being interested in the plot, the rats or the children; what stirred me deeply was hearing *real* singers and a *real* orchestra. The scenery and lighting were stunning. It was 1909, when I was seven, and I couldn't eat my dinner or sleep that night. I had taken my first deep drink of the heady wine known as theatre.

A musical show called *Little Nemo* did nothing to lessen my thirst. It was based on a comic strip running in one of the newspapers and had a delightful score by Victor Herbert, which I heard my parents play and sing for weeks until I knew every note and word. Finally the great day arrived, and I was taken to a Saturday matinée at the New Amsterdam Theatre, my first visit to a real Broadway house. I was so impressed that I still know exactly where we sat: the second box from the stage on the left side. That magnificent theatre is now a grind house on shabby Forty-second Street, but then—a sister theatre to the lovely Colonial Theatre in Boston—it provided an elegant setting for Victor Herbert's exciting and tender score, with lyrics by Harry B. Smith. I can still remember a seagoing march called "Give Us a Fleet" and a children's love song, "Won't You Be My Playmate?"

Early in 1910, without any warning, disaster struck. One night I awoke screaming with pain; the maid came running in and I showed her my right index finger. She took one look at it and said, "Oh, my God!" It was flame-red and swollen almost to the thickness of my wrist. There was nothing she could do, since my parents were at the theatre. I had to lie there, writhing with pain, and wait for my father and mother to come home. Neither of them panicked. Pop simply got a scalpel from his office and had Mom hold me while he made one terrifying slash in the finger to allow the pus to escape. (This was the first episode in a horror story that lasted for many months.) The next day my father took me to a surgeon friend of his whose office was nearby. Local anesthetic was seldom used in those days, and so what followed were eight months of torture to a small boy by well-meaning men whose scientific knowledge was still limited.

As bad as the pain was the fact that my whole world—playing the piano—stopped. My right arm was in a sling all those months, and there was no way for me to play the piano or even run with the boys in the street. All I could do was wait in terror for the next visit to the doctor. The wound had to be kept open, I was told, and one time I heard the word "blood poisoning," and another, in a whisper, "amputation." I was spared both of these because my father finally arranged for me to be seen by Dr. A. A. Berg, a famous surgeon at Mt. Sinai Hospital. Dr. Berg easily attracted notice because he always wore a bright-red tie, but his fame rested on the firmer foundation of being something of a surgical genius. I was taken to the operating room and placed on a table while Dr. Berg started to inject cocaine (this was before the Novocaine era) into my finger. Even here my luck ran out. The needle broke and Dr. Berg, cursing, threw the syringe on the floor. A new one was brought and the pain stopped. Minutes later he withdrew something from the inside of the finger. The prize he found was a piece of bone about a quarter of an inch square, very thin, with a pitted surface. No one ever discovered what caused the disease, which, I was later told, went by the romantic name of osteomyelitis. Two weeks later the wound had healed and my arm was out of a sling. The finger was a mess, however, and awful to look at, to say nothing of the fact that playing the piano was still almost impossible.

A year later my father took me back to Mt. Sinai, where Dr. Berg performed what may well have been one of the earliest plastic operations: he fashioned a new fingertip for me. It is not a thing of beauty, but the important thing was that I could play the piano again. Any lack of brilliance in my playing today is not due to that illness but to the fact that technically I am just not very proficient, though good enough to communicate musically anything I have to say. The only difficulty I have, however, is due to that operation; the tip of my index finger is a little bit thicker than it should be and the space between the black keys on a Knabe is too narrow. This creates a problem that Knabe and I have managed to live with for many years.

I have always had a tendency toward hypochondria, which I try to control, but I have often wondered if this is the result of that operation for adenoids, or of a loving father suddenly appearing in the middle of the night to cut me savagely with a knife.

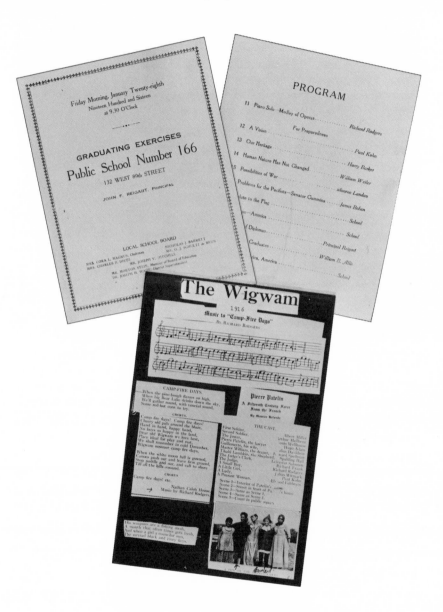

2

With the healing of my finger, a new phase in my life began. I was nine years old when I discovered that I could devise my own bits of melody. The appropriate harmonies were no trouble, since I already played quite well by ear. Soon I was writing complete tunes of my own. I don't remember that the family expressed any particular surprise; I suppose they just took my music for granted, something I certainly did not. I knew I gained deep satisfaction, both emotional and mental, from making up my own pieces. Of course, this was nothing more than improvising, but what is composition but formal improvisation? Certainly I was on my way, and from then on I never wanted to do anything else with my life.

About that time I recall many lengthy family discussions concerning the changes taking place in the neighborhood. Suddenly there was talk about a new apartment building about to be erected on Eighty-sixth Street between Amsterdam and Columbus avenues. The new building would have space on the street floor where my father could have his office, and a large apartment on the fifth floor where we all could live. There was one more maid's room than we needed, and this would be mine. I would also share a bathroom with the cook. It was further decided that my grandfather's room would be adjacent to mine so that I could go in and wake him up whenever he had one of his frequent nightmares and yelled in his sleep.

The move to Eighty-sixth Street meant another change of schools. This one was P.S. 166, between Amsterdam and Columbus avenues on Eighty-ninth Street. It was a good school, with what my mother considered a "better class" of boys. This meant that there were fewer tough kids and less chance that I would get into fights. At the end of each half-term there was always the big crisis of who would be "left back"—a huge disgrace—and who would be "skipped," a great honor. Being skipped meant saving a half year's work, a dispensation conferred only on very bright boys whose deportment was as good as their scholarship. One year, to my amazement, my teacher, Mr. Supnick, skipped me! Since I was never much of a student, the triumph was unbelievable, and the family seemed more impressed with this achievement than they had ever been with my music.

Nevertheless, it was my music that gave me status in the school and one more push in the direction of a career. The head of the music department was Elsa Katz. She was young, slim and attractive, but best of all, she liked me and was sympathetic to my musical efforts. She even gave me the task of playing all the music for the daily assemblies, an assignment usually carried out by middle-aged teachers who knew the technical rudiments of the piano but were uninterested, bored and wooden in performance. My job was to play the entrance and exit marches (my own improvisations), the traditional hymns and "The Star-Spangled Banner." Occasionally I made a musical joke. Whenever the principal said, "Students, sit," I would play the familiar musical doggerel "Shave and a haircut." Then, as the students sat, I'd play "Two bits." The kids never reacted, but lovely Miss Katz would always giggle.

Late in 1911 my grandfather took me to the Park Theatre, on the site in Columbus Circle now occupied by the Coliseum, to see a musical called *The Quaker Girl.* Ina Claire was the star, and I found out what it was like to fall in love with a real live actress. But beautiful and beautifully equipped though she was, I was too young and too innocent even to daydream about her. I never dared to tell this story to Ina, even when we became friendly in later years; I simply could not bring myself to say the most crushing sentence an actress can hear: "I was taken to see you when I was a child."

The Little Theatre is located on West Forty-fourth Street and is the smallest theatre in the Broadway district. My grandfather took me there the following year on another matinée excursion, this time to see Marguerite Clark in *Snow White and the Seven Dwarfs.* This time I was not intimidated by the age or the glamour of the leading lady. Miss Clark, who later became a star in silent pictures, was very young, extremely pretty and—what pleased me most—just about my size. All this made me fall so deeply in love that I spent many sleepless nights thinking about her. My prepubescent fantasies were restricted by my innocence, but as I look back on them I realize I was doing very well mentally for a ten-year-old and was clearly heading in the right direction.

With the usual logic of parents, mine decided a couple of years later that it was time for me to go away for the summer. With the usual lack of logic of parents, instead of choosing a conventional boys' camp, they decided on a place called the Weingart Institute. My guess is that they picked this particular place because the boys didn't sleep in tents, exposed to the ravages of the mild Catskill Mountains air. We were all housed in one large building that looked like a typical Catskill boarding house. I had a roommate named Bob Fisher. We didn't get along well and, frankly, I can't say that I was the most popular boy in the establishment. It may have been my personality, or it could have been that in a large group of average kids, my piano playing made me the pet of visiting parents and sisters.

I was at Weingart's in the summer of 1914, but the war in Europe was far too remote to mean anything to me or the other campers. We were involved in sports like tennis and swimming, and I was caught up in my own wonderful world of music. But there was something else; I was impatient to find out more about that grand but terrifying feeling which came over me whenever I was near a girl.

I graduated from P.S. 166 late in January 1916, and at the commencement exercises I did something only a thirteen-year-old would have the nerve to do. Without ever having seen a printed note of the music, I played a medley of operatic tunes by ear. The applause was satisfactory, and no one hissed. I didn't know enough to be grateful.

Before graduation, the family had held lengthy discussions at the dining table concerning the right high school for me. The public school with the highest standing was Townsend Harris Hall, known as T.H.H. It was a recognized fact that largely because it was a three-year school instead of the customary four, T.H.H. was the most difficult school in the city. I should have realized that it wasn't for me, but since my brother, Morty, had gone there, I figured if he could make it, I could too. To my surprise, I was admitted.

There was not much difficulty at first. I was too busy running for office —first for secretary of the athletic association, later for treasurer of the student government, better known as the G.O. By custom, boys running for office in the G.O. put up hand-lettered posters all over the school, but with the financial help of my father and brother I had *printed* posters all over the place. On the day of the election, Morty and his two best friends, Harry Phillips and Ralph Engelsman, went up to school, which was on the City College campus, and electioneered vigorously for me. How much persuasion and how much coercion they used I'll never know, but I was elected.

This victory was responsible in part for my downfall at Townsend Harris, and started a pattern I was to follow for the rest of my scholastic life: I always devoted too much time to nonacademic matters.

My grandmother and grandfather were great opera lovers and had Wednesday-night seats in the third row of the orchestra at the Metropolitan. One night my grandmother decided to stay home and let me go in her place. The opera was *Carmen* and the stars were Caruso and Geraldine Farrar. Giorgio Polacco conducted. Not being able to see the musicians in the pit, and never having heard a large orchestra before, I had no idea what to expect, but when Polacco brought his baton down on those first crashing figurations of the introduction, it was so overpowering that I thought I was going to faint. I recall that the Michaela was sung by Edith Mason, a young, lovely-looking girl who later married Polacco. Years later their daughter played one of the nuns in *The Sound of Music.*

Thanks to my grandparents I also saw the Diaghilev ballet with Pavlova and Nijinski. A few years later I stood in the back of the orchestra at Carnegie Hall to hear the great Josef Hofmann play the Tchaikovsky Piano

Concerto No. 1 in B-flat Minor. As soon as I heard the electrifying orchestral opening and the surging melody carried by the piano, I was as overcome
as I had been on my first evening at the opera. My knees buckled and I had
to hold on to the brass rail to keep from falling.

Because of this early love for classical music my career might easily
have developed in that direction, but the musical theatre always remained
my first love, perhaps because my mother and father had reached me before
anyone else.

In the summer of 1916, two years after my sojourn in the sheltered
atmosphere of Weingart's Institute, I was sent to a real boys' camp, tents
and all, in Harrison, Maine. Camp Wigwam was owned by Arnold Lehman
and Abraham Mandelstam, nicknamed Pop and Mandy. Pop was easygoing, but Mandy and I were troubled by a generation gap; I think I was too
old for him. But we did have one thing in common: he loved music and used
to invite first-rate musicians to perform at the camp. The one I recall most
fondly was a pianist named Arthur Loesser; he never condescended to us,
but played, tirelessly and sensationally, hour after hour. Years later I found
out from Frank Loesser that Arthur was his uncle. Talent obviously ran in
that family.

One of the counselors at Wigwam was a six-footer named Robert
Lippmann, then an undergraduate at Columbia. He was a great piano
player who played my kind of music, and he was also a gifted composer.
But most important, he was sympathetic and encouraging despite what
seemed to me a vast difference in our ages. Actually, it couldn't have been
more than four years.

It was at Camp Wigwam that I wrote my first real song. I have no idea
where the lyric came from, but the piece was called "Camp Fire Days" and
obviously extolled the joys of spending the summer at Dear Old Wigwam.
There was another song which I did not write. It was strongly discouraged
by the two camp owners but sung joyously in secret to the tune of "My
Bonnie Lies Over the Ocean." Since Pop and Mandy are no longer in a
position to disapprove, I reproduce here the elegant lyrics:

> To Wigwam we go in the summer,
> The lousiest place on this earth.
> For this we pay three hundred dollars,
> Which is fifty times more than it's worth.
> Bring back, bring back,
> Oh, bring back my money to me, to me.
> Bring back, bring back,
> Oh, bring back my money to me.

The Standard Theatre at Ninetieth Street and Broadway was part of the "Subway Circuit," a group of theatres that booked shows in Manhattan, Brooklyn and The Bronx after their Broadway runs. It was at the Standard that I saw my first Jerome Kern musical, *Very Good Eddie.* In the cast were Georgie Mack (who had succeeded Ernest Truex), Earl Benham (who later became a successful tailor), Ada Lewis and Helen Raymond. They were all good, but it was the Kern score that captivated me and made me a Kern worshiper. The sound of a Jerome Kern tune was not ragtime; nor did it have any of the Middle European inflections of Victor Herbert. It was all his own—the first truly American theatre music—and it pointed the way I wanted to be led. On Saturday afternoons I would take my allowance and get a seat in the balcony or gallery of a Subway Circuit or Broadway theatre to see and hear whatever musicals were being shown. If it was a Kern musical, I'd see it over and over again. I must have seen *Very Good Eddie* at least a half dozen times, and even lesser-known Kern, such as *Have a Heart* and *Love o' Mike,* enticed me back more than once.

Most of the successful early Kern shows, such as *Very Good Eddie, Oh, Boy!, Leave It to Jane,* and *Oh, Lady! Lady!!,* were known as Princess Theatre musicals, in honor of the tiny theatre where all but *Leave It to Jane* first opened. Most of them were written in collaboration with Guy Bolton (co-librettist) and P. G. Wodehouse (co-librettist and lyricist). They were intimate and uncluttered and tried to deal in a humorous way with modern, everyday characters. They were certainly different—and far more appealing to me—from the overblown operettas, mostly imported, that dominated the Broadway scene in the wake of *The Merry Widow* and *The Chocolate Soldier.*

Jerome Kern's orchestral arranger for most of these early shows was Frank Sadler. Here again was something new. Sadler used comparatively few musicians, and his work was contrapuntal and delicate, so that the sound emanating from the orchestra pit was very much in the nature of chamber music. The lyrics floated out with clarity, and there was good humor as well as sentiment in the use of instruments. Actually, I was watching and listening to the beginning of a new form of musical theatre in this country. Somehow I knew it and wanted desperately to be a part of it.

While I was struggling along at Townsend Harris, my brother was applying himself diligently to his studies at Columbia University. Columbia interested me too, but not from an academic point of view. All I knew was that the big nonathletic event of the year was the annual Varsity Show. *Home, James* was the name of the 1917 production, and one Saturday afternoon Morty took me to see it at the Astor Hotel Grand Ballroom.

Home, James was a lot of fun and had a number of attractive melodies written by my friend Bob Lippmann. The neatly turned lyrics, I noted, were the work of a prelaw student with the impressive name of Oscar Hammerstein II, who also had a part in the show. Even I knew that anyone named Oscar Hammerstein II had to be a member of one of New York's most illustrious theatre families.

When I told Morty how much I admired what Hammerstein had contributed, my brother, who was in the same fraternity as Oscar, offered to take me backstage to meet him. Going backstage at a Varsity Show was heady stuff for a fourteen-year-old stagestruck kid, and I was overawed when I was introduced to the worldly upperclassman who had not only acted in a Varsity Show but had also written its lyrics. Hammerstein was a very tall, skinny fellow with a sweet smile, clear blue eyes and an unfortunately mottled complexion. He accepted my awkward praise with unaffected graciousness and made me feel that my approval was the greatest compliment he could receive. No deathless words were exchanged at that first meeting, but it was an occasion that years later prompted an extended disagreement between us. Oscar insisted that I wore short pants that day while I, with equal certainty, stoutly maintained that I had already graduated to "longies."

That afternoon I went home with one irrevocable decision: I would also go to Columbia and I would also write the Varsity Show. I also decided that I couldn't waste much more time before starting out in my chosen profession. I was introduced to a young would-be lyricist named David Dyrenforth, and together we created something called "Auto Show Girl." We fully expected that that topical title would guarantee the song's popular appeal; needless to say, it didn't. It was, however, my very first copyrighted song. The date was June 30, 1917.

By the end of the term it became abundantly clear that T.H.H. and I were not meant for each other. My grades were getting worse and worse, so I decided to quit before I flunked out. Because DeWitt Clinton High School was known to be comparatively easy, I got a transfer, and in the fall of 1917 I entered that cathedral of learning. The building was at Fifty-ninth Street and Tenth Avenue, on the edge of a rough neighborhood then known as Hell's Kitchen.

Clinton's charm started at the front door and pervaded the entire building; it was the faint but unmistakable scent of men's room. Schoolwork was duller than ever, and I couldn't even find other kids to raise a little hell with. The musical and dramatic activities were minimal. I was saved from total boredom, however, by my English teacher, who told me that I could buy a single Saturday-night subscription in the balcony of the Metropolitan

Opera House for only $17. That Croesus of medicine, my father, came up with the money without a question, so my Saturday nights were happy ones filled with magnificent music. Still, much as I enjoyed opera, neither my attention nor my ambition was ever diverted from the field of musical comedy.

My grandparents, Rachel and Jacob Levy in the early 1900's

My mother (1892)

My father (1896)

My first picture (1902)

With my brother, Morty (1905)

Mother and child (circa 1908)

Oscar Hammerstein and Larry Hart at Columbia (circa 1916)

Going over the script of *Poor Little Ritz Girl* (1920)

With Morty at Camp Paradox in the summer of 1920

The team of Fields,
Rodgers and Hart
(1927)

FLORENCE VANDAMM

A publicity shot at the
ornate piano used in the
film *Love Me Tonight*
(1932)

PARAMOUNT

With Maurice Chevalier on the *Love Me Tonight* set

PARAMOUNT

Vacationing in Palm Springs with Dorothy, Moss Hart, Harry Brandt and Larry (1932)

Dorothy's wedding portrait

PACH

Mom and Pop with our daughter, Mary, in California

A duet with Mary, California (1933)

HARLAN THOMPSON

Mary and Linda (1937)

3

I wrote my first complete musical-comedy score in the fall of 1917. My brother was then a member of a local social-athletic group called the Akron Club. By that time the American Expeditionary Forces were fighting alongside the Allies against the Germans, and the boys of the Akron Club were anxious to do their bit to help the war effort. This, they decided, would be the production of an original musical comedy whose proceeds would go to a tobacco fund set up by the New York *Sun* to purchase cigarettes for our troops overseas.

The next problem was who would write the show. It was agreed that Ralph Engelsman, Morty's good friend, would be responsible for the book, but when it came to choosing a composer, the Akron boys discovered that they didn't have any members with the necessary talent. Since Ralph had been to our house frequently enough to hear me banging away at the piano, he suggested that I provide the songs. Apparently this produced some argument because of my tender age, but Ralph's enthusiasm carried the day and the club voted to accept me. This acceptance, I might add, was limited to writing the music for the show; at fifteen, I was still too young to become a member of the club.

The lyrics were another matter. I had no lyric-writer, so my father helped, my brother helped, Ralph Engelsman helped, and I contributed at least as much as they. Rehearsals lasted for months in small hired halls in the West Eighties and Nineties, or in the living rooms of cast members' parents. It was exciting to hear my melodies sung by talented young people, even though they were amateurs. Since hiring a pianist would have been expensive, I played at all the rehearsals and learned a great deal about vocal ranges and the proper keys to use.

The big night of the opening came on December 29, 1917, in the middle of a roaring blizzard. The single performance of *One Minute, Please* took place in the Grand Ballroom of the Plaza Hotel before a packed house of friends, relatives and other victims. I conducted an orchestra of five professional musicians and played the white-and-gold grand piano at the same time. I have no idea whether it was really a good show or not, but I thought it glorious. It was my first chance to examine the relationship between writing and audience reaction, to learn that what appears to be one thing on paper often undergoes a mysterious change in performance. This, I later realized, is really the answer to the question we are continually asked in the theatre: "How could such a smart man produce anything as bad as that?" The answer is that he simply does not know what he has until a live audience tells him. It is not a question of guessing; the producer, writers and composer all try to know in advance what the end result will be when the written word or note comes to life in front of human beings with their all too imponderable reactions.

Learning something about this metamorphosis began for me with the Akron Club show and I still wish I had solutions for some of these inherent problems.

A second amateur show, *Up Stage and Down,* gave me a little more experience. Sponsored by an organization called the Infants Relief Society, it played one night, in March 1919, in the Grand Ballroom of the old Waldorf-Astoria Hotel at Thirty-fourth Street and Fifth Avenue. Because I was still without a steady partner, I was again obliged to write most of the lyrics myself. My brother not only helped but also secured two new recruits to set words to my music: Benjamin Kaye, a theatrical lawyer who was my father's patient and a family friend, and Oscar Hammerstein, whom I had seen occasionally since our first meeting three years before. Hammerstein, now actually in the professional theatre as a stage manager for his uncle, producer Arthur Hammerstein, contributed the lyrics to three songs. For the record, they were called "Can It," "Weaknesses" and "There's Always Room for One More."

The show marked the first publication of my songs, an event hardly as impressive as it may sound, since my father paid the printing costs and I published them myself. We even managed to sell a few copies in the lobby.

As with the Akron Club show, I acted as both rehearsal pianist and conductor. One morning during a rehearsal Morty burst in and beckoned me away from the podium. When we were alone, he whispered, "The guys in charge don't think you're good enough to conduct. If they pull anything, pick up the music and walk out. If anyone tries to stop you, I'll murder him." Fortified by this homicidal insurance, I simply refused when the officers of the club later came to me and asked me to step down. This somehow ended the crisis, but I doubt that I would have had enough courage to take a stand without Morty's brave words.

About two months after its single performance, *Up Stage and Down* was revised and reopened for one night at the 44th Street Theatre. Now it was called *Twinkling Eyes,* for God's sake, and the beneficiary of our warmed-over efforts was the Soldiers and Sailors Welfare Fund.

Having written two complete musical scores, I saw no reason why the world should experience any further delay in appreciating my talents. Dorith Bamberger was a very pretty little girl whom I used to see fairly regularly and fairly innocently. Her mother, a widow, liked theatre music and even liked me. Trying to be of help, she took me to see an old friend of hers, Louis Dreyfus, who with his brother, Max, owned T. B. Harms, Inc., the Tiffany of the music-publishing business. Every Broadway composer of any consequence was under contract to Harms, including my hero, Jerome Kern. Mr. Dreyfus received us cordially, listened attentively to my tunes and gave me the exact advice I didn't want to hear: "Keep going to high school and come back some other time." Since I had no other choice, I kept going to high school. Later I did go back to Harms, though under somewhat different circumstances.

Fortunately, I received a bit more sympathy in other quarters. Though he was pleased that I had chosen a musical career, my father, a cautious man, still wanting to make sure that I wasn't making a mistake, took me to play for patients and friends whom he considered more knowledgeable than he was. One of them, Leonard Liebling, who had recently become the editor of *Musical Courier* magazine, was most kind and understanding. Another and even more important influence was Nola Arndt, the widow of composer Felix Arndt and the inspiration for her husband's famous piano piece, "Nola." Not only did Mrs. Arndt encourage me to go on with my music, she also gave me invaluable advice. "Don't be a so-called serious composer," she told me. "That's no life for you. And don't try to be a Tin Pan Alley songwriter, either, because you don't think that way. The place for you is the Broadway theatre. I think you'll find it more rewarding in every way than the concert hall or the popular-song field." I was also happy to learn that Mrs. Arndt was a great admirer of Jerome Kern and that she urged me to follow in the direction he was leading. Everything she said rang a loud, clear bell for both me and my parents.

I knew what I wanted to do and I knew where I was heading, but I also knew something else: every song needs words. I did not feel I was sufficiently adept at lyric-writing and I had not met anyone who I thought was. In my search for a partner I buttonholed almost everyone I knew for suggestions. Surprisingly, it didn't take long before someone did come up with the right name.

Phillip Leavitt, a classmate of my brother's at Columbia, was another one of the older boys who didn't patronize me but took my music seriously. One day he told me that there was a very good lyric-writer named Lorenz Hart, a Columbia graduate, who was looking for a composer. He explained that while Hart had had some peripheral experience in the professional theatre, he realized, as I did, that a writing partnership was of major importance in succeeding in the musical-comedy field.

Hart lived at 59 West 119th Street, just around the corner from where

I had spent my childhood, but we had never met. Early one Sunday afternoon Phil Leavitt and I rode the subway uptown, climbed the brownstone
steps of the house where the Harts lived, and rang the bell. We were greeted
by Lorenz Hart himself—Larry from then on. His appearance was so
incredible that I remember every single detail.

The total man was hardly more than five feet tall. He wore frayed
carpet slippers, a pair of tuxedo trousers, an undershirt and a nondescript
jacket. His hair was unbrushed, and he obviously hadn't had a shave for
a couple of days. All he needed was a tin cup and some pencils. But that
first look was misleading, for it missed the soft brown eyes, the straight nose,
the good mouth, the even teeth and the strong chin. Feature for feature he
had a handsome face, but it was set in a head that was a bit too large for
his body and gave him a slightly gnomelike appearance.

Larry was immensely jovial and led us into the back parlor, where
there was a large round table, a good console phonograph, and near the
window, an old upright piano. A cat ambled into the room and Larry
introduced us. "This is Bridget," he said. "She's an old fence-walker." He
chuckled at his joke and rubbed his hands furiously together, a nervous
habit he repeated frequently. Suddenly I heard a crashing *BONG!* that lifted
me out of my chair. Larry told me not to be frightened; it was only his
mother's clock sounding the hour.

To calm my nerves, Phil suggested I play some of my tunes. The piano
turned out to be in excellent shape, and Larry responded to my music with
extravagant enthusiasm. Then we talked. And talked. And talked. Actually,
Larry did most of the talking while I listened with all the reverence due a
man of twenty-three from a boy of sixteen. Larry's previous writing had
consisted almost solely of translating the lyrics of German operettas for the
Broadway producing firm of Lee and J. J. Shubert. Only they weren't mere
translations; they were actually adaptations, and excellent ones, for which
he was paid almost nothing. In place of cash he got a small lifetime of
experience, and as I listened I realized that here was a man who knew the
musical theatre and how to write for it. His theories, and they were count-
less, began with his disdain for the childishness of the lyrics then being
written for the stage. He felt that writers were afraid to approach adult
subject matter and that the rhyming in general was elementary and often
illiterate. His point was that the public was being cheated by writers who
mistrusted the audience because their own level of intelligence wasn't very
high to begin with.

Larry talked about a lot of things that afternoon, including arcane
matters of his trade, such as interior rhymes and feminine endings, that I
had never heard of before. But what really brought us together was our

mutual conviction that the musical theatre, as demonstrated by the pioneering efforts of Bolton, Wodehouse and Kern, was capable of achieving a far greater degree of artistic merit in every area than was apparent at the time. We had no idea exactly how it could be done, but we both knew that we had to try. As I wrote in a magazine article many years ago: "I left Hart's house having acquired in one afternoon a career, a partner, a best friend, and a source of permanent irritation."

It wasn't long before I became acquainted with the entire Hart ménage. Larry's parents, Frieda and Max, had come from Hamburg, Germany, and both spoke with thick accents. Teddy, Larry's kid brother, looked something like Larry and had an unforgettable high squeaky voice. Later he would become a fairly successful actor. There was also Rosie, the cook, who had one bad eye but a great talent for German food, and of course Bridget, the fence-walker.

Mrs. Hart was a darling woman, tiny and sweet-faced, who talked very quietly. She used to call us for lunch by saying, "Boys, der shops iss retty." And mighty fine "shops" they were, too. I don't know if she really had any idea what Larry and I were trying to do; her role in life seems to have been nothing more than to be kind and helpful at all times to all people.

The real character was Mr. Hart. He was no taller than Larry but must have weighed in at close to three hundred pounds. He seemed to have no neck, only a chin that descended in a gentle curve to his stomach. Just to hear him talk was an experience in itself. Besides a pronounced lisp, his language—not just his English, but his language—was incredible; he was vulgar beyond belief. One night when I was still a newcomer *chez* Hart, we were served lentil soup. Mr. Hart lifted a spoonful of the thick liquid about eight inches above the plate and poured it back in. "Frieda," he roared, "it lookth like—" "Mox!" Mrs. Hart screamed while Larry and his father yelled with laughter.

Mrs. Hart had some lovely old-fashioned jewelry and the family owned three automobiles. Periodically, however, Mrs. Hart had no jewelry and there were no automobiles to be seen. I learned later that everything was always being put up as collateral in some new business of Mr. Hart's. Before I knew him, Mr. Hart had been involved in any number of companies that mysteriously went bankrupt. Larry collected the letterheads of all of these companies. I don't suppose any other lyricist can claim the distinction of writing his first songs on the back of stationery of the Pittsburgh and Allegheny Coal Company.

Larry loved to tell the story of his father warning him and Teddy that they must fast until sundown on Yom Kippur. Around noon the boys passed Pomerantz's Delicatessen on Lenox Avenue. Through the window they saw Mr. Hart not only wolfing an enormous sandwich but enjoying it in the company of a large blonde. It was some years later that I found out that beneath all this nonsense was a kind, good-hearted man who loved his family but had never learned to behave himself.

This was equally true of Larry. The difference, of course, lay in the fact that Larry had a talent so great that it overcame the lack of discipline in his work and the lack of control in his life. I soon discovered that he could never work in the morning because he never felt well enough to concentrate. This was because he loved carousing to all hours of the night. The first drink, before lunch, helped, but by early afternoon he needed more help, and by late afternoon the working day was over.

Incredibly, my parents never expressed any objections about Larry. If he was the partner I wanted to work with, it was all right with them. The only comment I can recall my mother ever making occurred one day soon after we had met. Larry had come over to our apartment, and though ostensibly there to work, was more interested in helping himself to whatever liquor he could find. After he left, my mother said sadly, "That boy will never see twenty-five." He was twenty-three then, and while Ma's estimate was off by twenty-two years, it was apparent that the seeds of self-destruction had already been planted.

Often when I arrived at Larry's house he was upstairs trying to get himself together so that we could begin work. This meant a long wait alone in the parlor, and to pass the time I would play the phonograph. There were two recordings that I particularly loved and would play over and over. One was the first movement of Tchaikovsky's Fourth Symphony (the remaining three movements were missing), and the other was Rimsky-Korsakov's *Scheherazade.* War horses though they may be, they were vigorous and highly romantic, and they further stimulated a musical appetite in me that was already pretty healthy.

Throughout the spring and summer of 1919 Larry and I wrote a number of songs we weren't ashamed of, and by August we felt we were ready to audition some of our better efforts. Phil Leavitt, who had brought us together, now took it upon himself to bring us together with a producer. That summer the Leavitt family had rented a house in Far Rockaway next door to Lew Fields and his family. Fields had first won renown as one half of the great comedy team of Weber and Fields, which had convulsed audiences during the late nineteenth century. Though he had long since split with Joe Weber, he was now well established as both a solo comedy star and a producer.

With Phil's enthusiasm paving the way, one sweltering Sunday afternoon I journeyed to the Fields' summer home to unveil the first Rodgers and Hart songs before their first audience.

Though the audition was a major opportunity to break through into the ranks of Broadway songwriters, Larry, claiming a splitting headache, begged off. I would soon discover that whenever it came to "selling" or negotiating, he would always find some reason not to be available.

Lew Fields, a man of medium build, with a deeply lined face, sad eyes and a flat nose, greeted me at the door. Expecting to play my songs before an audience of one, I was surprised to find the entire Fields clan assembled to appraise my maiden efforts. In addition to Mr. and Mrs. Fields, the family consisted of their four children: Joseph, the eldest, who bore a close physical resemblance to his father; Herbert, wavy-haired and clean-cut looking; fourteen-year-old Dorothy with the most dazzling eyes I had ever seen; and Frances, the only Fields sibling who would not pursue a career in the theatre. All six of them did what they could to make me feel comfortable, though I must admit that most of the time I found myself trying harder to impress young Dorothy than her father. When I had finished, I felt a genuine sense of accomplishment in hearing so many favorable comments from so knowledgeable a group, and I would have considered my trip worthwhile even if I had nothing more concrete than admiration and encouragement to take home with me. It turned out to be a little more than that.

Lew Fields was then starring at the Casino Theatre in a musical called *A Lonely Romeo,* which he also produced. I was stunned and slightly hysterical when he said that he would not only buy one of our songs, "Any Old Place with You," but also find a spot for it in *A Lonely Romeo.* I fumbled my thanks and appreciation, danced out of the house and rushed to the nearest public telephone to break the news to my father. "Pop," I began, trying to be funny, "I have some terrible news . . ." And then I told him what had happened. Pop was almost as excited as I was—but not until after he had first given me hell for frightening the daylights out of him.

So it was that on August 26, 1919, at a Wednesday matinée, the career of Rodgers and Hart was professionally launched. It wasn't much of a splash, but to Larry and me Niagara Falls never made such a roar as the sound of those nice matinée ladies patting their gloved hands together as the song ended. The girl who sang it was Eve Lynn; the boy was a curly-haired towhead named Alan Hale who later became famous as a hard-hitting tough guy in Hollywood pictures.

For "Any Old Place with You," Larry took as his theme all the gay things a honeymooning couple might do, hopping from Syria to Siberia and from Virginia to Abyssinia, ending with the sure-fire laugh getter, "I'd go to hell for ya,/ Or Philadelphia!" Since the lyric prescribed that this world-wide jaunt be accomplished via rail, I came up with a bouncy melody that was intended to simulate the carefree chug-chugging of a honeymoon express. It was all pretty naïve, I suppose, but we were sure that we had begun our career in the most worldly and sophisticated manner possible.

I don't believe "Any Old Place with You" had the stuff of which hits are made, but what mattered to us was that a song we had written was being performed in a Broadway show and that audiences were enjoying it. Now we were sure nothing would stand in our way. Our path was blocked many times and in a variety of ways, but we never knew enough to quit.

I have found time and again that not knowing enough to quit is one of the most important factors in theatrical success. A lot of improbable people have made it to the top, not by talent alone but simply because they were there. Young people often come to me for advice about ways of breaking into the theatre. My answer is always the same: "Take a job, any job, that will get you inside a theatre. Be an usher, be a 'gofer' [someone who goes for sandwiches and cigarettes], be anything. Sooner or later the chances are that the impossible will happen: you'll get a job as an assistant stage manager, or they'll give you a walk-on with one line, or you'll be tapped to replace someone in the chorus. A good agent—if you can get one to take you on—can be of help, but the most important thing is to be where the action is."

4

By the fall of 1919 I was too miserable at DeWitt Clinton to continue there any longer. Columbia University was offering certain courses in "extension," which made it possible to attend freshman classes even though I had not finished high school. But what appealed to me most was that I would be accepted as a freshman socially and could write the Varsity Show—provided, of course, that I won the competition. Since eligibility requirements were obviously lax, Larry Hart also qualified to write the Varsity Show, although he had been out of Columbia for three years.

So I became a member of the class of '23 in September 1919. The very first day I arrived on campus I found out about a singing contest to be held among the four classes, with each class expected to sing a traditional Columbia song. No sooner had I heard this than I decided that *my* class had to have an original song. I rushed home, wrote the words and music, rushed back, got the class together and taught the boys the song just in time for the contest. For the edification of all, here are the imperishable words:

> C boys,
>> it's '23 boys,
>> and
> O we'll give 'em
> L.
> U boys,
>> be true boys,
>> and
> M we'll make 'em yell!
> B boys,
>> forever steadfast,
> I will for
> A.
>
> (shouted)
> C-O-L-U-M-B-I-A!
>
> '23 Hurray!

We won the contest hands down and I became the class hero. From then on, the only other freshman who approached me in fame was a chubby little fellow named Edward Roche Hardy who got his picture in all the papers because, at thirteen, he was the youngest student ever to have been accepted at Columbia.

Early in 1920 I was an extremely busy lad. First there was another commission from the Akron Club—this time, naturally, with Larry Hart as collaborator. *You'd Be Surprised* was the title of the show, which the program proudly proclaimed "An 'atrocious' musical comedy." It probably was, despite our corralling the services of three members of the Fields family. Lew Fields was credited for "Professional Assistance," Dorothy played one of the leads, and Herbert contributed the lyric to a show-stopping number about "poor bisected, disconnected Mary, Queen of Scots." The musical played the Plaza Hotel Grand Ballroom the night of March 6.

Exactly eighteen days later Larry and I had our second musical of the year, *Fly with Me,* which opened at the Astor Hotel Grand Ballroom. But *Fly with Me* wasn't just another amateur show; it was the Columbia Varsity Show of 1920.

Beyond doubt, the Triangle Show at Princeton and the Hasty Pudding Show at Harvard were classier ventures, because Princeton and Harvard were classier schools. But the Varsity Show at Columbia offered a boy like me something no other school in the country could supply: an almost professional production. There were experienced directors, a beautifully equipped stage with good lighting situated in the heart of the Broadway theatre district, and best of all, professional musicians in the pit. Here, certainly, were near-ideal working conditions; here, possibly, was an opportunity that could be of incalculable help in furthering my career.

Since writing the Varsity Show had been the sole reason I entered Columbia, one of my first priorities when I got there was to look for a suitable musical-comedy idea. Somehow Larry and I got hold of a libretto by another student, named Milton Kroopf, who promptly disappeared out of my life, and we turned the script over for revisions to our matchmaking friend, Phil Leavitt. The book was a gag-filled fantasy set fifty years in the future (in 1970!), and our locale was an island—Manhattan, of course—that was then ruled by the Soviets. Once the writing had been completed, we submitted the show to three Varsity Show judges, Richard Conried, Ray Perkins (later a comedy writer and radio personality) and Oscar Hammerstein II, whose first musical, *Always You,* was then playing on Broadway. After due deliberation the judges chose *Fly with Me* as the Varsity Show over the four other entries submitted.

Rehearsals began in January in the basement of one of the Columbia buildings, with Herb Fields staging the dances and a professional actor, Ralph Bunker, directing the book. As rehearsal pianist, I had to spend endless hours banging out the tunes on a tinny upright, but since the tunes were mine, I loved doing it. The lyrics were all Larry's except for Oscar Hammerstein's "There's Always Room for One More" and "Weaknesses," which we lifted from the *Up Stage and Down–Twinkling Eyes* score.

About a year before *Fly with Me,* Roy Webb, a Columbia alumnus, had taught me the rudiments of musical notation and conducting. Roy had also written Varsity Shows as a Columbia undergraduate, and I found him to be not only experienced but exceedingly patient and kind. It was largely his training that gave me the confidence I needed when, on the morning of the first orchestra rehearsal, I went up to the Roof Garden of the Astor and bravely faced the seasoned Broadway musicians of "my" orchestra. It must be highly rewarding for a painter to see his paintings exhibited, or for a writer to come up with a best seller, or for a business executive to complete a successful deal, but I cannot imagine anything more thrilling than standing on a podium leading—*leading*—a group of professional musicians playing your own music. I've always understood why the boy who is elected president of his class makes up his mind that eventually he will run for the Presidency of the United States. Early achievement creates a thirst hard to satisfy. In my own field, that thirst began with my early experience of writing theatre scores and then conducting them before large and enthusiastic audiences.

Fly with Me, which gave the first of its four performances at the Astor on March 24, was somewhat better than an amateur show, as the term is generally used. It had a large chorus of burly college men—in drag, of course—many of whom sang beautifully, some genuinely comic performers, and an entire company of passionately hard workers. In addition, the professional contributions of our director and our musicians helped give the show a near-professional look and sound. I must also say that Larry Hart, Herb Fields and I brought a good share of expertise to the construction, rehearsing and eventual performance. (Incidentally, despite a cast of talented players, we three were the only ones to seek careers in the professional theatre.)

Since Lew Fields considered Larry and me something of a personal discovery, and since his own son was involved in the production, it was only natural that he would attend a performance of *Fly with Me.* What certainly was not natural was that he was so impressed with the music and lyrics that, almost on the spot, he decided to hire Rodgers and Hart to write the score for his next production.

This was unbelievable. There I was, a seventeen-year-old college freshman, and one of the theatre's most respected producers wanted *my* songs for a major Broadway show. Even Hollywood wouldn't have dared invent that one. But it happened, though the occasion turned out to be somewhat less auspicious than I had expected.

What Larry and I didn't know at first, but would soon find out, was that Lew Fields, thoroughly dissatisfied with the score created by a team he had already hired, was desperately searching for a replacement. A number of valid reasons led to his choosing us. First, having seen *You'd Be Surprised* and *Fly with Me,* he was impressed with our ability to come up with the kind of score he wanted. Secondly, since his forthcoming production—and I can no longer withhold the fact that it was called *Poor Little Ritz Girl*—was already booked to open its Boston tryout in May, he thought he could save time by using some of the songs from our two most recent efforts. Lastly, since he had to pay off the original writers, he figured, correctly, that we would be so thrilled at the opportunity that we would willingly accept a lower fee than a team with professional experience.

But none of this detracted from our excitement, apprehension and pride in actually writing a complete Broadway score. We worked in a Broadway theatre, the Central (now the Forum), at Forty-seventh Street and Broadway. There were real live chorus girls, seductive-looking but too intimidating to touch, and experienced theatre people were all over the place. Going through the stage door each day, I became familiar with the smell peculiar to stage doors. It isn't a pleasant or unpleasant odor; it simply means Theatre. Even today I still get that stirring of excitement, that feeling of venturing into the unknown whenever I go through a stage door and smell that combination of canvas, paint and wood.

The story these experienced theatre people had come up with was a simple-minded affair dealing with a chorus girl—of the *Poor Little Ritz Girl* company—who innocently rents the apartment of a wealthy young bachelor while he is out of town. He returns unexpectedly, and . . . well, you can take it from there.

Rehearsals went uneventfully for Larry and me simply because no one paid much attention to us. Once we had submitted our songs they were out of our hands. Eventually the big moment came when, trying hard to act like seasoned professionals, we boarded the night train to Boston with the rest of the company for the world premiere of *Poor Little Ritz Girl.* The next morning when we got off, my aplomb was thoroughly shattered when I discovered that we had lost Larry. It seems that he was so small that the porter couldn't find him in his upper berth to wake him in time, so he slept his way out to the train yards. He didn't make it to the theatre until the afternoon.

Poor Little Ritz Girl was the first attraction to play the new Wilbur Theatre. It opened to encouraging reviews, both for the show and for the score. Though most of the songs were written specifically for the production, we did, as originally planned, use some of the numbers from our last two amateur musicals. "The Boomerang," "Mary, Queen of Scots" (which got the biggest hand) and "Will You Forgive Me?" (previously known as "Princess of the Willow Tree") had been in *You'd Be Surprised.* We also borrowed three numbers from *Fly with Me,* though all were outfitted with new lyrics: "Peek in Pekin" became "Love's Intense in Tents," "Dreaming True" became "Love Will Call," and "Don't Love Me Like Othello" became "You Can't Fool Your Dreams." This last was considered particularly original in that its theme—"You tell me what you're dreaming, I'll tell you whom you love"—may well have been the first song with a somewhat Freudian philosophy.

With such capable actors as Victor Morley, Lulu McConnell and Roy Atwell in the leads, we were all reasonably optimistic about the show's chances on Broadway. The opening, however, was not scheduled to take place until the end of July. Since there was nothing else to do for the moment, I accepted a job as a counselor at a boys' camp called Camp Paradox. It was run by a likable fellow named Ed Goldwater, who hired me primarily to compose songs for a series of Sunday-night shows put on for the entertainment of campers, parents and friends. Herb Fields was also a counselor there, and putting these shows together was great experience as well as fun.

Still, it was murderous not to be with my show during its tryout tour. What was worse was the lack of communication. I had no idea what, if any, changes were being made, and I relied on the supposition that someone would let me know if anything radical was being done.

Getting Ed Goldwater's permission to go to New York for the opening was easy. Actually, I was given the send-off of a conquering hero-to-be, and I thought of nothing but my impending triumph as I lay sleepless in my berth on the midnight train heading for New York. In the morning I rushed straight to the theatre—and received the bitterest blow of my life. Half of our songs had been cut and replaced by numbers written by the more experienced team of Sigmund Romberg and Alex Gerber. Not only that; the story had been changed (Lew Fields was now crediting himself as co-author), Charles Purcell and Andrew Tombes had replaced Victor Morley and Roy Atwell, and a new girl was playing the title role. They had even hired a new musical director, Charles Previn.

What had happened, of course, was that despite some critical indications of success, the show had not really been in good shape in Boston and had not attracted customers. So Fields simply obeyed the ancient show-business dictum that is still all too often followed today: If something is wrong, change *everything!*

Naturally, Larry and I were in no mood to be philosophical or to see any reason for a situation that ironically was something of a reversal of the one we had experienced in *A Lonely Romeo.* When our one song had been added to that show, we were thrilled at our luck and had no qualms that it might be improper to interpolate it into someone else's score. But with *Poor Little Ritz Girl* we were the original writers, and it seemed at best inconsiderate and at worst deceitful to add a total of eight numbers without even giving us an inkling of what was going on. And these weren't merely additions, they were actual substitutions. This is what hurt most of all.

The Broadway opening of *Poor Little Ritz Girl* was July 28, 1920, and even now, more than fifty years later, I can still feel the grinding pain of bitter disappointment and depression. I didn't want my parents at the opening, but since there was no way to keep them out, we sat and suffered together until they took me to the train to go back to camp—one badly bruised unconquering hero.

In fairness, I must admit that most of the changes were improvements. The Romberg tunes, though not especially original, were energetic and helpful to this sort of piece, and the cast replacements were wisely made. My father even became fond of an innocent phallic joke: "You never can tell the depth of the well by the length of the pump handle."

I was particularly surprised at the reviews, which Pop sent to me at camp. While Rodgers and Hart weren't exactly being hailed as the new white knights of Broadway, the show itself received generally favorable comments. In the New York *Tribune,* Heywood Broun wrote: "The average musical comedy is copied after the one which was produced the month before. *Poor Little Ritz Girl* may serve to break the endless chain. It shows an effort to put an ear to the ground rather than at the crack of the stage door across the street." Much to Larry's chagrin, however, the song most singled out for praise, "Mary, Queen of Scots," had words by Herb Fields. Alan Dale, the critic of the *American,* claimed it was worth the price of admission, though he loftily admonished that "some of the profanity could be advantageously deleted. H—l is no longer funny. It's merely silly."

The show ran for nearly three months, which was pretty good in those days. Today, of course, a three-month run would be disastrous, but in 1920 a Broadway production needed no more than six months to make it one of the major hits of the season. In fact, the competition *Poor Little Ritz Girl* faced made its run all the more remarkable. Theatregoers could take their pick of such fare as *The Night Boat,* with a delectable Jerome Kern score, the latest *Ziegfeld Follies* with Fanny Brice and W. C. Fields, a Hippodrome spectacle featuring girls disappearing into a tank of water, the second edition of the *George White's Scandals* (and the first to boast a Gershwin score), and Oscar Hammerstein's latest effort, *Tickle Me,* starring comedian

Frank Tinney. Best of all was *Irene,* a holdover from the previous season, with a charming score by Joe McCarthy and Harry Tierney, including "Alice Blue Gown."

Even though I now considered myself a full-fledged Broadway composer, in the fall of 1920, I did what any teen-ager is expected to do: return to school. Again all I wanted to do was to write the next Columbia Varsity Show, and again I was chosen to do it. It was called *You'll Never Know,* and I haven't the foggiest recollection of what it was about. I do know, because I still have the program, that it was co-authored by Herman Axelrod (whose son, George, became a successful playwright), that it was co-directed by Oscar Hammerstein, and that its dances were staged by Herb Fields.

Herewith I submit a list of titles of musical comedies:

You'd Be Surprised

Fly with Me

Say Mama!

You'll Never Know

Say It with Jazz

The Chinese Lantern

Jazz à la Carte

If I Were King

A Danish Yankee at King Tut's Court

Temple Belles

The Prisoner of Zenda

These frequently ridiculous names represent the musicals for which I wrote scores between 1920 and 1924. I cite them because since all eleven were amateur shows, they provide the best answer I can give to a question I have been asked repeatedly: "How does anyone get started in show business?" My point is that there is a great deal more to writing for the musical theatre than learning notation, the meaning of a diminished seventh, or banging away at a typewriter in some lonely room. My advice is to reject at the start the idea that "amateur" is a dirty word, and to remember that while the qualitative differences between amateur and professional productions may be vast, the resemblances are equally great. Both require singers, actors, lighting, scenery, costumes, musical accompaniment and eventually an audience. On the way to that audience, writers, whether amateur or professional, are constantly polishing and making changes; through trial and error they learn what makes dialogue funny or touching and what makes a song not only suitable but remembered.

As a showcase, the amateur production can even have immediately practical results. In the audience may be someone's uncle who knows an agent or a producer—or who may even *be* an agent or a producer—and the amateur may have taken the first giant step toward becoming a professional.

This isn't just wishful thinking; it happened to me. Because Lew Fields saw a couple of amateur musicals by Rodgers and Hart, we had been signed to write the score for *Poor Little Ritz Girl.* Even though that was a professional effort, Larry and I quickly discovered that every step was the same as in the amateur shows we had been doing. The transition was smooth simply because we had already been through the required mental and physical discipline necessary for any stage production.

5

In 1920, most of my social life was spent with two girls. I have already mentioned Dorith Bamberger, whose mother had tried to be helpful by introducing me to Louis Dreyfus. The other girl was named Helen, and no matter how innocent we managed to keep our relationship, it was pretty daring for those days, since she was already married. Because her husband was continually away on lengthy business trips, it was possible for us to spend many hours together, mostly walking in Central Park discussing our two favorite topics, ourselves and music. Helen, who wasn't much older than I was, had no technical knowledge of music, but she had a passion for it equal to mine and an understanding far greater. She was many things to me—teacher, mother, confidante and companion. To listen to Brahms with her was a deeply emotional experience that added an extra dimension to my already all-consuming love for music.

Both Dorith and Helen had unbounded faith in my ability and were forever dreaming up ideas about the best ways I could prepare myself for that inevitable day when all Broadway would be singing my songs. Since neither girl knew the other, it seemed a significant coincidence that each of them suggested at about the same time that I should quit Columbia as soon as possible and transfer to the Institute of Musical Art, the most prestigious music school in the city (it still is today, but now it is known as Juilliard).

I was well aware that academically Columbia had little to offer me in the area in which I was concentrating all my interest. I had already achieved my scholastic goal of writing two Varsity Shows, and therefore considered myself eligible for graduation right then. My idea of heaven was a place where I would be surrounded by nothing but music, so the girls didn't have a hard job selling me on the idea.

But I dreaded the next step: telling my father. Pop was not only a college man but a strong believer in the importance of a well-rounded education. While I was grateful for his encouragement of my musical career, I had my doubts that he was ready to give his blessing to my chucking the higher academic life in favor of a specialized school. I should have known better. Pop's reaction was typical of the way he treated me as long as he lived. He listened quietly while I got the whole thing off my chest, and when I was all through my carefully rehearsed speech, he simply said, "If that's what you feel you should do, do it."

I don't suppose anybody ever went into music with less opposition or more encouragement than I. We've all heard stories of the young songwriters who have succeeded in spite of strong parental disapproval, but I cannot recall a single instance when there was even the slightest hint from my parents that I was wasting my time. The only opposition I was ever aware of came from my grandfather, even though he was a great music lover and inveterate opera goer. I have no idea where he developed the fixation, but he repeated it as if it were gospel: "Even if you are successful, they'll never pay you."

With Pop's and Mom's approval, and despite Grandpa's warning, I happily abandoned my losing struggle with geometry and French and enrolled in the Institute to learn all I could about the vastly more appealing world of music. This turned out to include just about everything except mastering an instrument, since I soon discovered that my piano playing would never be any better than adequate. (I did, however, study what was known as "secondary piano," a course usually taken by students of singing or those who majored in other instruments.) What really excited me and made me certain that I had chosen the right educational path were the lectures and the courses I took in music theory, harmony and ear-training.

Franklin W. Robinson conducted special classes in music theory, but a more appropriate name for them would be musical aesthetics. The topic may sound dull, but Mr. Robinson, who was a well-known church organist as well as teacher, had a way of making it fascinating. For instance: "The next time you go to the Philharmonic, listen to a fellow named Bruno Labate who plays the oboe. Then you will really understand what the word 'concert' means. Here is a man who plays like a soloist but always plays *with* the orchestra. Besides that, he's an exquisite musician." Thereafter, whenever I went to the Philharmonic I paid particular attention to Mr. Labate and his oboe. He was a little guy and very fat, not pretty to look at but mighty pretty to listen to. He alone taught me a great deal about music in performance.

I was fortunate to be a member of a class in harmony taught by Percy Goetschius, who was to harmony what Gray was to anatomy. He had a wonderful sense of humor and was very easygoing, his only unbreakable rule being that he would not teach more than five students at a time. Whenever Goetschius talked about ending a phrase with a straight-out tonic chord (the first, third and fifth step of any scale), he would call it a "pig," his term for anything that was too easy or obvious. Once I heard the scorn in Goetschius' voice I knew that I'd avoid that "pig" as if my life depended on it.

Ear-training was another course that sharpened my understanding of music. My teacher, George Wedge, who later became dean of the Institute, conducted these classes more like fun and games than serious academic work. By this time I had already learned how to make my own piano transcriptions (which I still do), but it was a revelation to learn that by some curious kind of musical magnetics, the fourth step of the scale was pulled down to the third, and that the seventh was pulled up to the eighth. Nobody has ever explained it scientifically, but if you take the simple phrase of the music that goes with "Shave and a haircut, two bits," you'll find that the note that goes with "two" is carried, whether it wants to or not, to the note that goes with "bits." It's almost impossible for it to go anywhere else.

In addition to regular classes, the Institute offered stimulating lectures by the leading musical authorities of the day. One of my favorites was Henry Krehbiel, the music critic of the New York *Tribune* and probably the foremost critic in the country. Whenever he was scheduled to talk, I would leave home a half-hour earlier in order to make sure of getting a front-row seat. By just listening to him expound on Beethoven, you actually heard Beethoven. As he spoke he would become so emotional that tears rolled down his long red beard. After a lecture by Krehbiel, a Beethoven symphony or sonata was a brand-new experience, as if I were listening to it with a new pair of ears.

I never got to know him well, but Frank Damrosch, the founder and director of the Institute, was always sympathetic about my ambitions, and had a surprising knowledge and appreciation of the commercial musical theatre. Dr. Damrosch *was* the Institute: he set the tone, created the atmosphere and established the traditions. One of these was the ritual of the final exams; they always took place in the evening, with the entire faculty attending in formal dinner jacket and black tie.

Another was the year-end musical revue that kidded both the school and the music world in general. Here at last was a chance for the Institute's only Broadway-bound composer to shine! In fact, my first show, *Say It with Jazz,* was such a hit that I'm convinced I won scholarships for my second and third years just to make sure that I'd be on hand to write the shows. *Say It with Jazz* was based, more or less, on Rimsky-Korsakov's *Coq d'Or.* I contributed new songs written with Larry Hart and, for insurance, a few of the better applause getters which I had written for previous amateur efforts.

For the Institute's 1922 show, *Jazz à la Carte,* we had the services of Herb Fields to stage the dances and help direct the scenes, and William Kroll, a masterly violinist who later founded the Kroll String Quartet, as musical director. Gerald Warburg, my closest friend at the Institute, also contributed a few songs. Gerry was the son of Felix Warburg, the banker and art patron. His greatest love was the cello, which he played beautifully, and like all the members of his family, he managed to combine a vocation in finance with an avocation in music. In addition to new songs, for this show I also included such tested numbers as "There's Always Room for One More" and the hit of the evening, "Mary, Queen of Scots" (done as a takeoff on Maria Jeritza in *Tosca*). The following year, under the influence of Mark Twain and the recently discovered tomb of the Egyptian king Tutankhamen, we offered something called *A Danish Yankee in King Tut's Court*. Again it was mostly a Fields, Hart and Rodgers production.

I loved my years at the Institute. I could devote myself completely to something I cared for deeply, and for the first time in my life I was surrounded by students and teachers whose addiction to music was as great as mine, even though their interests were primarily confined to the concert hall or the classroom. A good many of the students who were there went on to become famous soloists, but the majority went to the Institute to study pedagogy before returning home to teach. Because I was the only pupil there whose goal was to write for the musical stage, I felt a bit self-conscious at first in being among people whose aims in life were, at least by tradition, considered loftier. But it didn't take long before I realized that my fellow students didn't look down their noses at someone whose aim was the tinseled world of Broadway. From teachers and classmates alike I can recall nothing but an attitude of mutual help and respect, and I'm sure that's why, for the first time in my life, I was actually learning something in a school. It may be true that some men thrive on opposition and are inspired by antagonism, but I've never been one of them. I cannot conceive of being in any kind of a personal relationship based on conflict, whether teacher–pupil, husband–wife, friend–friend, or partner–partner. In school, I learned well only from teachers who were lax in discipline but firm in sympathy and understanding, and for the most part, this is what I found at the Institute.

My whole experience there was more like an adventure than going to a school. My feeling of excitement and anticipation began in the morning when I got on the subway at Eighty-sixth and Broadway for the ride up to 116th Street. By the time I reached Claremont Avenue and 122nd Street, where the building was located, I could scarcely keep from running. When I returned home late in the afternoon I was fairly bursting with stories of the wonders I had discovered during the day. There isn't the slightest doubt that my years at the Institute were far more beneficial to me than four years at college could possibly have been.

Much as I was devoted to the Institute, I never let anything keep me from seizing opportunities to get ahead in my chosen field. Perhaps to make up for my disappointing experience with *Poor Little Ritz Girl,* Lew Fields again offered me a chance to work in the professional theatre—though not as a composer and not on Broadway. During the summer of 1921, he had appeared in a Broadway revue called *Snapshots of 1921*. It wasn't much of a hit, but it fitted into the plans of Lee and J. J. Shubert, then New York's leading theatre owners and producers. Anxious to set up their own vaudeville circuit to compete with the one operated by B. F. Keith, the Shubert brothers decided on a slightly different format. Instead of following the customary practice of booking individual acts that went from city to city, the Shuberts' plan was to send entire entertainments on tour. The first half of each unit would be the customary vaudeville acts, and the second would be a truncated, or "tab," version of a recent Broadway revue. Counting primarily on the box-office attraction of the Fields name, the Shuberts chose *Snapshots of 1921* as one of the attractions to be cut down and sent out that fall, and Lew Fields chose me as the musical director of the show.

Actually, I wasn't with the show from the beginning. *Snapshots* had already started on tour when Fields sent for me to replace the original conductor, who had signed on for only two months. I arrived in Pittsburgh in December 1921 to study the show, which would require my services both for *Snapshots* and for the various vaudeville acts that preceded it. In each city the unit played, there was an orchestra rehearsal on Monday morning, followed by the show's opening that afternoon. My debut as a professional conductor took place at the Shubert-Detroit Opera House. Once I had recovered from my initial nervousness, I found that the musicians were as cooperative and as helpful as those I had worked with on my amateur shows. I learned a lot about keys, tempos and the various ways an orchestra could help a singer project a song. I also learned a lot about life beyond the confines of an orchestra pit. Working in cities like New Haven, Toronto, Buffalo, and Chicago was exciting for a nineteen-year-old kid whose only other experience living away from home had been limited to summer camps.

Among the vaudeville acts traveling with us I recall only two. The first was Belle Story, who had been a leading singer at the New York Hippodrome. She had a lovely coloratura voice and made a big hit wherever we played, particularly with her singing of "The Marriage of the Lily and the Rose." The other performer I remember was a thin young man with an odd nasal voice and a sad face with prominent pouches under his eyes. He played the banjo and sat on the edge of the stage with his legs dangling into the orchestra pit. He was a superb deadpan comic, a fact that would become even more widely appreciated when Fred Allen became a coast-to-coast radio favorite.

Snapshots closed on the road in the spring of 1922 and I returned to my studies at the Institute of Musical Art. I also went back to writing amateur shows. One of these was a musical version of Justin Huntly McCarthy's celebrated swashbuckler, *If I Were King,* which had to do with the way the poet François Villon saved Paris by becoming king for a day. Herb Fields, Larry Hart and I collaborated on this effort, which was written for a benefit sponsored by the Benjamin School for Girls. All the characters in the production were played by the school's students including, in the role of Villon, Dorothy Fields sporting a beard.

Somehow, possibly through Lew Fields, a Broadway producer named Russell Janney heard about our production. He sent for me, I auditioned the numbers, and he was enthusiastic enough to say that he thought they would be just right for a Broadway adaptation. Shades of Lew Fields and my first Columbia Varsity Show! Janney never went so far as to offer a contract or discuss terms, but his sincerity was obvious and I was convinced that Rodgers and Hart would soon again have their names associated with a professional show.

So I went home and waited for Janney's call. And waited. And waited. With a what-have-I-got-to-lose feeling, I eventually called him. He mumbled an apology about not getting back to me, and then explained the facts of Broadway life: his associates—that is, financial backers—were unwilling to risk money on any project, no matter how worthy, that had been created by writers so young and inexperienced.

"But don't *you* think it can be a success on Broadway?" I pleaded.

"Yes."

"And don't *they* think it has merit?"

"Yes."

"Then why can't we go ahead?"

"They won't take a chance."

It was the same routine I had experienced with *Poor Little Ritz Girl,* except that at least there I ended up with half a score. Now, almost three years later, I was being treated as an even ranker amateur. I had already shared songwriting credit with Sigmund Romberg for a moderately successful Broadway musical; I had studied at the leading music school in the city; I had toured as musical director of a vaudeville unit for the Shubert brothers; I was constantly composing songs for whatever school, synagogue or club wanted to sponsor a musical comedy or revue. Yet I was still being told that I lacked experience. And how was I to gain more experience without being given the chance to work in the professional theatre?

Surely, I felt, Janney should have more faith in his own taste. He wouldn't be the first one who did. What about that young producer Alex Aarons? In 1919 he had given a twenty-year-old piano-pounder named George Gershwin a chance to write the music for a show called *La, La, Lucille.* Now Gershwin had the assignment to write all the songs for the annual *George White's Scandals*. A couple of years before, Aarons had discovered another composer, Vincent Youmans, and hired him for *Two Little Girls in Blue*. Now Youmans, at twenty-four, had one of the biggest successes in town with *Wildflower*. And not only did both composers have show hits, they also had song hits—Gershwin with "Swanee" and "I'll Build a Stairway to Paradise," and Youmans with "Bambalina."

I tried to console myself with the knowledge that Gershwin and Youmans were both about four years older than I. But the fact was that they didn't have any reputation when they were given their first break on Broadway—nor did they have to suffer, as I had, the indignity of a well-known composer being rushed in at the last minute to decimate their scores. What's more, they were able to capitalize on their maiden efforts and to go on almost immediately to establish themselves among the foremost writers in the musical theatre.

Two and a half years after Janney had shown enthusiasm for the Rodgers and Hart *If I Were King*, he did get to produce the story as a musical, and true to the convictions of his financial supporters, he engaged an experienced and successful composer, Rudolf Friml, to write the score. Since the show, now retitled *The Vagabond King*, became one of the triumphs of the decade, I don't suppose Janney ever had any cause for regret.

So *If I Were King* ended in frustration. But I couldn't waste time brooding, particularly when Herb Fields and Larry Hart had come up with a really novel idea for a musical, which might even be timely today. In the story, our hero invents a kind of "electronic" system that obviates the use of electric wires for communication and electric power. The locale is a small city called Winkle Town (which was also the name of the play), and the plot deals with the hero's attempt—ultimately successful, of course—to convince the town fathers that the idea is both practical and beneficial.

Somewhere in the course of writing the book, we felt that the story line wasn't working out as well as we had hoped. We needed help and, almost on a dare, we went to Oscar Hammerstein. He had already established himself on Broadway with six productions—including the current hit, *Wildflower*—so we weren't counting on more than a word or two of advice. But Oscar not only read the script, he liked the concept and the songs so much that he agreed to join us as collaborator.

As it turned out, he was unable to spend much time with us, nor was he able to lick the book problems that were still plaguing us. Nevertheless, I took the completed script and all the songs I had written to a young producer named Laurence Schwab whose first show, *The Gingham Girl*, had been a big hit the previous year. I don't recall how I got the introduction to Schwab, though I do recall that he liked the songs but hated the book. By this time we had all more or less given up on *Winkle Town,* so there were no objections from Herb, Larry or Oscar when I came up with a new proposal. Knowing that Schwab was about to go into production on a musical he was writing with Frank Mandel, and also knowing that he still hadn't chosen a composer and lyricist, I offered him the use of our *Winkle Town* songs as the basis of the score for his new show.

Schwab, however, said that while he thought he might be able to work the songs into his libretto, he didn't consider his judgment regarding their merit expert enough, so he asked me if I would mind playing them for a good friend of his, Max Dreyfus of T. B. Harms. Of course I didn't mind, though I was still a bit rankled by my previous visit to that company when Max Dreyfus' brother, Louis, had told me to go back to school.

I soon discovered that Max Dreyfus was no more of a diplomat than his brother. After ushering Schwab and me into his office, this aesthetic-looking titan of the music business sat with eyes half closed as I played my songs. When I had finished, Dreyfus slowly turned to Schwab and said, "There is nothing of value here. I don't hear any music and I think you'd be making a great mistake."

I was so stunned that I couldn't say a word. My heart began to pound violently and I felt the blood rush to my face. Nothing of value? He didn't hear any music? Oscar Hammerstein had thought so much of the score that he had joined us in writing the show. Before we met Dreyfus, Schwab himself had been impressed. Now, suddenly, with two sentences, the verdict was being handed down that I had no talent. I could understand Dreyfus liking some songs better than others; I could even understand his *hating* some songs. But he didn't like anything—not even the one song that had never failed to get a positive reaction, no matter on whom we had tried it out. This was a swinging, light-hearted ode to all the joys of living in New York which we called "Manhattan."

It didn't take long for me to appreciate the reason for Dreyfus' harsh judgment. The next thing he said to Schwab was, "You know, we have a young man here under contract to us who would be perfect for the job. His name is Vincent Youmans."

The end of this little story was, of course, that Larry Schwab did not hire Rodgers and Hart for his new musical. But he didn't hire Vincent Youmans, either. By the time the show, *Sweet Little Devil,* opened in New York early in 1924, the score was the product of Ira and George Gershwin. Needless to say, they too were under contract to Harms.

Obviously, plays with music cost a great deal more to produce than plays without music. Since we seemed to be having no luck in finding a sponsor with enough confidence in his own judgment and taste to take a chance on a musical written by a couple of still-struggling songwriters, Larry and I reasoned that we should next try something more modest, a comedy perhaps, which might have an easier time getting on the boards. At the very least it would get our names known in the profession, and we could always sneak in a song or two just to let everyone know the direction in which we were still heading.

So we hashed over a few ideas with Herb Fields and finally settled on a rather simple-minded sentimental tale which, I must confess, had about it the aroma of *The Music Master,* one of David Belasco's turn-of-the-century hits. Our plot had to do with an elderly Austrian immigrant composer who is forced to earn his living as an arranger for a Tin Pan Alley music publisher. When the publisher has one of the composer's serious pieces jazzed up as "Moonlight Mama," the old man is disconsolate. Thanks to the composer's daughter and a young violinist, there is a happy ending, and poor old Franz Henkel is at last free to devote himself to the kind of music he loves.

Because of the play's theme, we made sure to include a couple of songs: the jazzy "Moonlight Mama," naturally, and as something of a burlesque on the comic songs of the day, "I'd Like to Poison Ivy."

Herb, Larry and I all contributed to the story, taking turns at the typewriter and throwing ideas around. When we finished the manuscript, the three names looked rather unwieldy on the title page, so we decided to combine our first names and give all the credit to one "Herbert Richard Lorenz." This may have been the cleverest idea we had.

In creating the main character, we consciously thought of the role as a part that would be perfect for Lew Fields, but I must say that we were all a bit surprised when he not only agreed with us but decided to put the play into production. It was, I believe, the first time that he had ever appeared in a work that was neither a musical comedy nor a revue.

We opened the show in Bethlehem, Pennsylvania, in March 1924 and kept it out of New York for two and a half months. Originally it was called *The Jazz King,* then *Henky,* and finally *The Melody Man* (if anyone wanted to confuse that title with *The Music Master,* it was all right with us).

During the Chicago tryout, Fields made the shattering discovery that he didn't have enough money to bring the show into New York. We held a hurried meeting and decided that Max Hart, Larry's father, was the only person who knew where and how to find the missing $1,000, and that I was the only person who could talk him into doing the finding. So back to New York I went, saw Mr. Hart in his office and explained the problem. As soon as I finished, Hart picked up his telephone and called Billy Rose. Rose, only about a year older than I, had already made a sizable amount of money as a lyricist, and his connection with Hart was that on more than one occasion he had paid Larry to ghostwrite lyrics for which he took the credit. I sat and listened while Mr. Hart fed Billy a line in his lisping German accent about what a tremendous success the play was in Chicago and that he might just be able to use his influence to let Billy buy into the show for $1,000. I don't know whether Rose was really taken in by Hart's fairy tale or whether he did it as a favor to Larry, but the check was in the mail the next day.

With Billy Rose's $1,000, we managed to get *The Melody Man* to open in New York on schedule, but no amount of money could have kept it running very long. The reviewers applauded Lew Fields but used the backs of their hands for the efforts of Herbert Richard Lorenz. Perhaps George Jean Nathan put it best when he wrote: "The plot is not only enough to ruin the play; it is enough—and I feel that I may say it without fear of contradiction—to ruin even *Hamlet.*"

One good thing did come out of the unfortunate experience. The part of the play's hero, the violinist, was played by a handsome young man who had had a few years of acting experience under his real name, Frederick Bickel. For *The Melody Man,* however, he was persuaded to change it to the softer-sounding Fredric March. I got to know Freddie pretty well during our only professional experience together. Whatever he did on the stage was never less than highly professional, and usually a good deal more. But offstage we would talk for hours, not about ourselves or the silly play, but chiefly about conditions in the world and the state of the arts in general. He was extremely well read and had a deep social conscience which affected his philosophical outlook. Through the years, and especially after his marriage to the lovely Florence Eldridge, Freddie and I maintained a warm affection for each other that was always deeply satisfying. Nowadays we hear the term "Beautiful People" bestowed upon members of the fast-paced, fast-buck international set. They aren't beautiful at all. To me, the Beautiful People are those like Fredric and Florence March.

Larry and I were sure of one thing after *The Melody Man:* we were never going to make it in the musical theatre by backing into Broadway with a nondescript play and a couple of satirical songs. Succeed or fail, we would have to stick with what we knew and what we did best. All this comes under the heading of Experience. We were learning—painfully—our trade with all its inherent pitfalls and misjudgments. But enough was enough. Couldn't Experience include something successful for a change?

We also knew that we couldn't afford to lose much more time. No sooner had *The Melody Man* opened than Larry came up with an idea for a story, and promptly turned it over to Herb Fields to develop into the book for a musical. An omniverous reader, Larry had long been intrigued by the theatrical possibilities of an incident in the American Revolution, when Mrs. Robert Murray, after whose family Murray Hill was named, managed by her feminine charms to detain the British general, Sir William Howe, long enough for the American forces under General Putnam to flee lower Manhattan to join General Washington's army on Harlem Heights. It was a good story, which Herb embellished with the inevitable romance, this one between an English captain and an American girl, and it gave us ample opportunity for a variety of musical expressions. We called the show *Dear Enemy.*

Confident that we had at last come up with a potential winner, during the fall and winter of 1924–25 we made the rounds of producers and publishers—and heard the same old story. We were unknowns and no one wanted to take a chance on unknowns, especially when they'd written something calling for elaborate settings and costumes. Once again we were treated to the demoralizing sound of doors being slammed in our faces.

Surprisingly, though, along the way we did pick up two important allies. One was Helen Ford, a petite, attractive actress with a lovely voice, who had scored impressively in two hits in a row, *The Gingham Girl,* Larry Schwab's first production, and *Helen of Troy, New York.* We heard that Helen was looking for a suitable new musical, and somehow I managed to persuade her to let us audition our show. This was a slightly roundabout way of doing things, but I reasoned that once Helen Ford indicated her willingness to star in our musical, she could at best find us a producer or at least make it easier for us to find one.

Helen came to my parents' apartment one evening, met Larry and Herb, and listened to us sing the songs and read the scenes. She was a wonderful audience and praised almost everything she heard. When we were finished, we looked anxiously in her direction and were treated to the exact words we wanted to hear: "I'd love to play the leading part." The words that followed, however, were *not* what we wanted to hear: "Who's going to produce it and who's putting up the money?" We had to admit that we still had no idea, and she had to admit that she had no idea either, but she assured us that she would do everything possible to help. Nothing that night could dissuade us from our euphoric belief that with Helen Ford as our intended star every producer in town would be begging us for the chance to sponsor our show.

Helen had just closed in a short-lived musical produced by A. L. Jones and Morris Green, and she was quick to set up an appointment with them. They liked what they heard, but having just lost money on their last show, they were leery of—here we go again!—taking a chance on unknown writers. Fortunately they didn't stop there.

Ever since 1919, Jones and Green had presented an annual revue, *The Greenwich Village Follies.* Even though they did not feel they could handle our show at that moment, they were impressed enough to arrange a meeting for us with the director, John Murray Anderson, who turned out to be our second ally.

Anderson, a saturnine, elegant Englishman with sad eyes and a prominent jaw, was extremely encouraging after listening to the songs and an outline of the plot. He would very much like to direct the show, he told us, and would certainly help us find a sponsor. The only trouble was that at the time he was completely occupied with directing Irving Berlin's latest *Music Box Revue,* which, since it represented his first major Broadway assignment, required his total concentration. So that, for the time being, was that.

With nothing else to do, we continued our frustrating quest. One day Anderson called me to say that he had just hung up on a young scion of wealth who was anxious to take a fling in the theatre. Anderson had talked the man into agreeing to listen to our score, but the catch was that I had to audition for him that very evening. Did he want to read the script? No, not just now. Did he want Helen Ford there or any other singers? No, not just now.

As soon as the butler ushered me into the gentleman's fashionable Park Avenue apartment I discovered that our would-be backer was not alone; he was having a party. He drunkenly introduced himself and told me to go over to the piano and start playing. So I went over to the piano and started playing. It didn't take long for me to realize that the young man couldn't care less about my songs; all he wanted was someone to provide free entertainment for his guests. There must have been eight couples there, and while I played everyone was drinking, laughing and snuggling. Despite my irritation, I found myself fascinated by the scene, so I just kept on playing and looking. Eventually, after I had performed the score straight through, my host told me I could go home. Apparently by that time everyone was all set to provide his and her own entertainment.

The winter of 1924–25 was the most miserable period of my life. No matter what I did or where I turned, I was getting nowhere. I would get up each morning, take my songs to a producer or publisher I thought might be interested, audition them—or, more likely, be told to come back some other time—and go home. This happened day after day after day. After the drubbing he had taken with *The Melody Man,* Lew Fields turned us down.

Larry Schwab never returned my call. Russell Janney was busy with his production of *The Vagabond King.* I couldn't get past the reception desks at the Shubert and Dillingham offices. And I certainly wasn't about to approach Max Dreyfus again.

None of this really dampened my confidence in *Dear Enemy.* I still felt sure that the songs were original and attractive and had good commercial possibilities, and that the story was at least as strong as anything being done on Broadway. But it seemed that no one who agreed with me was able to do anything about it.

What made things even harder to bear was that Broadway was bursting with activity. That season Rudolf Friml had *Rose-Marie,* and Sigmund Romberg *The Student Prince.* There was also Irving Berlin's fourth *Music Box Revue,* and another spectacular *Ziegfeld Follies.* But I suppose what bothered me most was that my most celebrated contemporaries, George Gershwin and Vincent Youmans, had gone on to even greater achievements. One of the biggest hits was Gershwin's *Lady, Be Good!,* starring the stage's greatest dance team, Fred and Adele Astaire. In Chicago, Youmans' *No, No, Nanette* was being acclaimed even before its scheduled New York opening. It wasn't that I didn't like their music; next to Kern, there were no two composers I admired more, both for their rhythmic vitality and the freshness of their melodic ideas. But I also had confidence in my own ability, and I just couldn't understand why, in a season that could offer over forty musical productions, everyone else managed to get a show on the boards except Fields, Rodgers and Hart.

Because of this, I was troubled at the time by severe insomnia. At night I'd lie awake in bed, tortured by the feeling that I might actually be at the end of my career. For over seven years I had been composing scores for every possible type of musical show. I had been a boy wonder. I had even made it to Broadway at an earlier age than Gershwin. Once everything had seemed to be falling into place easily; now I was twenty-two and it all seemed to be falling apart.

Since I had dropped out of college to devote myself to composing for the theatre, and since it was apparent that the theatre was able to get along very nicely without me, the next question was, What to do now? The idea of becoming a music director had a certain appeal since I enjoyed conducting, but the thought of spending my life with other people's music turned me off. I knew I could never play well enough to become a professional pianist. What about teaching? Most of the students I had known at the Institute of Musical Art were now music teachers, and from what I heard it was a satisfying life. But what category of music would I teach? Did I know enough about *any* category of music to teach it? Was I qualified to do anything besides sit at a piano and make up melodies?

Adding to my worries was the fact that I was not alone. I had a partner who was dependent on me. Larry, however, never seemed to be much concerned about our string of misfortunes. He managed to take everything in his stride, and while he may not have been of any help in auditioning or negotiating, he was a great morale booster because of his unfailingly optimistic spirit. Throughout this entire time we never had one disagreement about what course we should follow, nor were there ever any words between us about who was to blame for our lack of progress.

Then there were my parents to consider. Seeing their daily look of concern and listening to their attempts to bolster my sagging morale only succeeded in adding to my feelings of frustration, bitterness and guilt—with guilt probably the strongest emotion. At an age when most fellows I knew were already settled in their careers, at a time when my own brother was poring over medical books and laying the groundwork for a lifetime in medicine, I wasn't earning a penny. It was this aching feeling of guilt that for a while actually turned me away from music; for weeks I wouldn't even go near the piano.

Life in the Rodgers household when I was a kid had been hell chiefly because of the friction between my father and my grandmother. Even though Grandma had been dead for four years, life was still hell. There was no bickering, no yelling, no tight-faced silence. Now it was hell because I hated myself for sponging off my parents, and I hated myself for the lies I would rattle off about this producer or that publisher being so impressed with my work that it wouldn't be long before everything would be just dandy. Not once did I ever hear Mom or Pop say a single word that was not sympathetic, or show in any way that they were not behind me in whatever I wanted to do. I couldn't even get rid of my raging frustration by accusing them of not understanding me!

With desperation and despondency churning within me, I felt that the time had come for me to restore some measure of self-respect by going out and getting a job. One night I happened to unburden myself to a friend of mine named Earl. He told me about a Mr. Marvin (I don't think I ever knew his first name), a wholesaler in the babies'-underwear business with an office directly across the hall from his own. Marvin, it seems, though unmarried and fairly young, was anxious to retire and was looking around for someone he could train to take over the business when he quit. It was a one-man operation, with Marvin doing all the buying, selling and traveling on the road.

Though I had no business experience in any field, nor any particular affinity for the babies'-underwear business, I found myself intrigued by the idea of applying for the position. Why not? It mightn't be bad at all. I'd be my own boss, travel around, see the country, build the business, make enough money to enjoy life. Then, who knows, maybe someday I'd give it up and go back to composing. Larry would still be around . . . Anyway, it would be a challenge; more important, I wouldn't have to duck around the corner every time I saw someone I knew coming down the street.

So, without telling Larry or my parents, I met Mr. Marvin. We hit it off immediately; even allowing for my lack of business experience, he seemed to feel I could handle the job. Before I left his office, Marvin had made me a firm offer, with a starting salary of $50 a week. There I was, on the brink of earning what was, to me, a fantastic amount of money—and yet something held me back from accepting. Though puzzled at my sudden indecision, Marvin agreed to give me until the following morning to make up my mind.

That night at dinner I received a telephone call from Benjamin Kaye, the theatrical lawyer who, besides having written a few plays, had collaborated with me on a song for *Up Stage and Down.* Since I hadn't spoken to him for some time, I was surprised at the call. I was even more surprised at the reason. Over the phone I heard Ben's gentle, unemotional voice say, "Dick, some of the kids from the Theatre Guild are putting on a benefit show. I told them you'd be just the right fellow to write the songs."

One important element of success in any field is knowing when to say yes and when to say no. Perhaps I should have realized that Ben's offer was finally going to lead to the break I needed, but that's hindsight. What actually happened was that with my head reeling from months of frustration and my current indecision about the business world, the only words I heard were "benefit show."

"Thanks, Ben," I said, and I felt my voice tightening, "but I've been through all that before. I'm not going to do any more amateur shows. I'm sick of wasting my time. I've been doing them for over seven years, and all they've ever led me to is a dead end." Then, trying to sound casual, I added, "Anyway, I've decided to quit the music field. As a matter of fact, I've just been offered an important position with a business firm."

"Well, all right, Dick, if that's the way you feel," Ben said, "but Terry Helburn and Lawrence Langner are going to be awfully disappointed. I really gave you a hell of a build-up."

"Terry Helburn and Lawrence Langner?" My voice must have gone up at least an octave.

"Yes, Terry Helburn and Lawrence Langner. I did say the Theatre Guild."

"Then this isn't going to be an amateur show?"

"Well, not exactly. The kids who are putting on the show are mostly bit players in Guild productions. About a year ago they got together and organized something called the Theatre Guild Junior Players, mostly to do experimental plays and put them on for the benefit of the Guild management. Terry and Lawrence have been very encouraging, and now the group wants to do something to show its appreciation. After kicking some ideas around, someone came up with the notion of putting on a musical revue to raise money to buy tapestries for the new Guild Theatre on Fifty-second Street. It'll be a great opportunity for a lot of talented kids to be noticed by the public. You won't be earning any money, but since Terry and Lawrence have given their blessing, the Guild itself is planning to sponsor it."

Ben didn't have to say another word. Under the leadership of Theresa Helburn and Lawrence Langner, the Theatre Guild had become the most prestigious producing organization in the country, offering its subscribers a rich, if slightly heavy, diet of plays by the likes of Strindberg, Shaw and Ibsen. The mere fact that this was going to be the Guild's first musical—even though it would be a semiamateur benefit show—was bound to stir up considerable interest. It would mean not only a sold-out house but an audience that would certainly include important theatre people as well as critics from the daily papers. In a way it would be my final test. If I couldn't make it with this kind of showcase, I'd know I couldn't make it, *period.* But I knew that I could—I *had* to. There would never be another chance like this. Obviously, the more I thought about the project the more I found it losing its amateur status and assuming the dimension of *A Theatre Guild Production.* By the time I got to sleep that night I was sure of one thing: the world was going to have to get along with one less tycoon in the babies'-underwear business.

Ben Kaye arranged a meeting for me with Helburn and Langner in their office. They were a charming but oddly contrasting couple. Terry was a tiny, birdlike little lady who always wore a hat and looked as if she'd be more at home sponsoring tea parties than some of the major dramatic works of the century. Lawrence was an erect, courtly chairman-of-the-board type who spoke with an attractively musical accent that revealed his Welsh origin. As I played my songs for them I had to keep reminding myself that these two warm, enthusiastic people were really the Theatre Guild and not doting relatives encouraging their favorite nephew.

It was as simple as that. I played, they liked what I played, and the job was mine. Literally overnight I was lifted from despair to being the first musical-comedy composer ever accepted by the Theatre Guild.

I soon found out, however, that there was one problem, and a major one. Prominent among the Junior Players was a bright, talented actress named Edith Meiser. Even before Ben called me, it had been understood that Edith would not only appear in the revue but would also write the lyrics for the songs. Although I was scarcely in a position to dictate terms, I was adamant on one point: I would compose the songs with no other lyricist than Larry Hart. Fortunately, after some discussion, it was agreed to accept Hart along with Rodgers.

But I hadn't taken into consideration Larry's unpredictability. He didn't want to do it. He, too, was tired of the old amateur grind, with nothing in the bank to show for it. The prestige of the Theatre Guild meant little to him, and he was unhappy about the lack of time we had to put the whole thing together. But what bothered him most was that the show, being a revue, required nothing more from us than a collection of songs. He was convinced that the only way we could win recognition was to create a unified score for a book musical, with songs written for specific characters and situations. I finally talked him into the assignment by proposing that we try to incorporate a short, self-contained book musical into the revue as the first-act finale.

Since the theatre we were to play in was the Garrick, on West Thirty-fifth Street, it was decided to call the revue *The Garrick Gaieties*, and since the current tenants of the Garrick were Alfred Lunt and Lynn Fontanne, in their memorable production of Ferenc Molnár's *The Guardsman*, it was further decided to schedule two performances on Sunday, the theatre's "dark" day, May 17, 1925.

All the rehearsals took place at the Garrick. Because of the limited time, we worked, ate and napped there. Sets and costumes were kept simple, and our lighting consisted of anything we could use from *The Guardsman*. I don't think the whole production cost more than $3,000.

Although I had worked with professional actors before, I couldn't help feeling that there was something special about this particular group. They were all young and talented, but they also had something even rarer: a combination of love, loyalty, dedication and ambition that was enormously stimulating. Terry Helburn and Lawrence Langner seemed to sense it too; they never patronized us or made us feel in any way that our efforts were any less worthy than their more serious endeavors.

Thinking back on those days conjures up so many quick impressions: Philip Loeb, our deceptively mild-looking director, who could have tamed a cageful of lions with a word or a glance; Lee Strasberg, an acknowledged authority on acting even then, auditioning with the incongruous choice of "My Wild Irish Rose"; Sterling Holloway, a floppy-haired string bean, who always sounded as if he couldn't utter a word without first swallowing it; Herb Fields, whom Larry and I had brought in as dance director, trying to find enough room to work out his routines on the same cluttered stage as the singers; Libby Holman (then Elizabeth Holman), who always insisted I didn't play low enough when I accompanied her.

One morning a plump, pretty girl walked into the theatre and asked me if she could play the piano for rehearsals. She didn't even care whether or not she'd be paid. Since I had my hands full supervising the musical numbers, accompanying the singers and dancers, and writing whatever new material was needed, I was grateful to be relieved of at least one of these chores—provided, of course, that she could play well enough. She proved it simply by sitting down and, from memory, giving a note-perfect rendition of the song I'd just played, down to the exact harmonies and rhythmic nuances. This remarkable girl was Margot Hopkins (then Margot Milham), who not only played for all the succeeding *Gaieties* rehearsals but continued to be my rehearsal pianist for almost every Broadway show I did.

The Sunday of our two scheduled performances finally came. When the houselights dimmed, I crawled up from under the stage and took my place facing the eleven musicians in the orchestra. The packed audience babbled and rustled programs during the overture and applauded perfunctorily when it was over.

The curtain rose on the first number, "Soliciting Subscriptions." Since ours was a satirical revue aimed primarily at puncturing the arty pretensions of the theatre—especially the Theatre Guild—we opened with representatives of three little theatre groups, the Neighborhood Playhouse, the Provincetown Playhouse and the Actors' Theatre, explaining what each one stood for and why it merited support. At the end the trio introduced the rest of the cast with *"The Garrick Gaieties* is coming down the street! Here's where we meet our meat!"* And out came the kids, all holding banners with the names of Theatre Guild successes, to explain—in "Gilding the Guild" —that they were there to raise cash to help beautify the Guild's new theatre. Happily, the number achieved the primary function of any opening routine: it gave the members of the audience an idea of what the rest of the show would be like and put them in a properly receptive mood.

The first sketch, written by Ben Kaye, satirized the Garrick Theatre's current tenant, *The Guardsman,* with Romney Brent as Alfred Lunt and Edith Meiser as Lynn Fontanne. It won laughs in all the right places from the theatre-wise audience, which showed that it was at least willing to meet us halfway. Ben had also written the lyric to the next song, "The Butcher, the Baker, the Candlestick-Maker," with music by his friend Mme. Mana-Zucca. It was a jaunty piece about a girl's dalliance with the three gentlemen of the title, and received an appreciative hand.

Edith Meiser's sketch, "The Theatre Guild Enters Heaven," again ribbed our indulgent sponsors with a scene depicting St. Peter (Romney Brent) and a heavenly jury passing on the moral acceptability of recent Guild heroines. Following a dance by Eleanor Shaler, Edith Meiser came out to sing "An Old Fashioned Girl," the lone effort of the team of Rodgers and Meiser. Edith had shown me the lyric during rehearsals, and since I liked it and Larry offered no objection, I wrote an appropriately waltzing melody for it. The song was a lament for the good old days when men were men, and according to Edith's inspired line, "thought Freud was just German for 'joy.'"

Not counting the opening number, the first Rodgers and Hart song in the show was "April Fool," sung by Betty Starbuck and Romney Brent. By now there was every indication that the audience was with us, and it wasn't simply because the customers were charitable toward the young or that the tickets were cheap. Though I couldn't see the people sitting in the dark behind me, I could actually feel the warmth and enthusiasm on the back of my neck. Our show was creating that rare kind of chemistry that produces sparks on both sides of the footlights. What the people were responding to was an irresistible combination of innocence and smartness, two qualities I'm sure helped make "April Fool" one of the best-received pieces so far.

There followed another Ben Kaye sketch, "They Didn't Know What They Were Getting," an adroit takeoff on Sidney Howard's play *They Knew What They Wanted*. A backstage trio, "The Stage Managers' Chorus," won only mild approval, but Hildegarde Halliday's impersonation of monologist Ruth Draper was a crowd pleaser.

Then came our first-act finale, "The Joy Spreader." Gilbert Seldes, the drama critic and playwright, had given us the idea, and the program credited him for being "primarily responsible for this outrage." Our "jazz opera," as it was billed, was set in a department store where a salesgirl (Betty Starbuck) and a clerk (Romney Brent) have been locked in for the night. The following morning they are confronted by the puritanical store owner, but eventually they prove young love to be both virtuous and victorious. Though I'm not sure the audience quite got the hang of an opera form written in popular style, everyone seemed to appreciate our attempt at something a little daring, and the curtain came down to an extremely generous hand.

Act Two opened with "Rancho Mexicana," a number off the geographical track of the rest of the show. It was a colorful, festive story-in-dance routine, and we included it because it offered us the services of both Rose Rolando, a dancer, and her husband, Miguel Covarrubias, a well-known artist, who had designed the sets and costumes. They also brought along their own authentic Mexican music. This was our one "spectacle," and it got the second act off to a rousing start.

"Ladies of the Box Office," which followed, kidded such current examples of theatrical femininity as Mary Pickford (Betty Starbuck), a Ziegfeld show girl (Libby Holman) and the Sadie Thompson character in *Rain* (June Cochrane). A sketch by Arthur Sullivan and Morrie Ryskind, "Mr. and Mrs.," was our lone excursion into political satire. The gag here was to have President Calvin Coolidge (John McGovern) chewed out by his wife (Edith Meiser) for spending a wild evening with Herb Hoover listening to the radio and coming home at the ungodly hour of ten. The audience roared at the sight of Coolidge taking off his coat to reveal both red suspenders and a thick red belt.

I had a sense of anticipation when we began the next number—the one Larry and I had written for *Winkle Town* which, except for Max Dreyfus, everyone who'd ever heard it liked immediately. "Manhattan" was staged simply "in one" (that is, before the curtain while the scenery was being changed behind) as a boy-girl duet for Sterling Holloway and June Cochrane. Its easygoing, strolling melody and ingeniously rhymed lyric related all of the everyday pleasures to be found in New York and didn't require literal or even stylized reproduction. Though the stage was bare except for two kids, the audience could see and feel everything the song conveyed, and they ate it up. June and Sterling had to give at least two encores, and they could have given more if we had written more. If one song can be said to have "made" Rodgers and Hart, it surely was "Manhattan."

"Where Credit Is Due," a sketch about product-plugging, followed, but I was still so excited at the reception for "Manhattan" that I have no idea how it went over. In fact, I almost missed my cue for "The Three Musketeers," a second holdover from *Winkle Town,* which was sung by Sterling Holloway, Romney Brent and Philip Loeb. It was a typical revue number of the time in that it took a well-known historical situation and kidded it with modern slang (e.g., "Athos, Porthos and Aramis/We are the kittens' pajamis"). Not the best or the worst of its kind, the song benefited greatly from the trio's inventive sight gags that made it much funnier than it really was.

Two more Rodgers and Hart songs followed: "Do You Love Me?," a quizzical ballad sung by Louise Richardson, and "Black and Blue," a torchy ballad moaned by Libby Holman. "Fate in the Morning," the last sketch before the finale, did a hilarious job of skewering still another arty Theatre Guild production, *Fata Morgana.*

After the finale—a full-company reprise of "Gilding the Guild," with new lyrics—the theatre was in an uproar. I turned around to look at the audience; everyone was standing. Not standing to leave, just standing. Not just standing, either. Standing and clapping, cheering, yelling, stomping, waving and whistling. I turned back to the orchestra and had the boys strike up "Manhattan." The cast sang it. The musicians sang it. Even the audience sang it. After about ten curtain calls, the houselights went on, but still no one wanted to go. At last, slowly and hesitantly, the audience filed out, as if unwilling to leave to memory an experience that was so vivid and exciting.

Tired, exultant and wringing wet, I rushed backstage, hugging and kissing everyone in sight. We were a bunch of kids who had worked like hell and were now enjoying the almost unbearable ecstasy of having everything turn out just right. Physiologically we may have been sober but emotionally we were all drunk, and there's no greater feeling than that.

All at once we were shatteringly brought back to reality. Larry was jumping up and down, rubbing his hands together and screaming, "This show's gonna run a year! It's gonna run a year!" We all looked at one another. It wasn't going to run a year; it wasn't even going to run another day. We had only one more performance, that very night, and then it would be all over.

The evening performance went just as well as the matinée. Again there was the feeling in the back of my neck that the audience, even when silent, was loving every minute of it, and again there was wild enthusiasm at the end.

The next morning's reviews confirmed everything that had happened the day before: "absolutely fresh in word, song, dance, skit, and bit of skittishness" . . . "went over like a bunch of firecrackers" . . . "brisk, refreshing and entertaining" . . . "a witty, boisterous, athletic chow-chow" . . . "bright with the brightness of something new-minted" . . . "as spontaneous and quick-moving a show as is to be found in town" . . . "full of youth, energy and fine flashes of wit" . . . "Rodgers and Hart's stuff clicked here like a colonel's heels at attention."

With such a reception, how could we possibly let *The Garrick Gaieties* die? I spoke to Terry Helburn and she was only too happy to give us the theatre for matinées the following week—except, of course, for the two afternoons that *The Guardsman* was playing. Despite the fact that this particular week was one of the hottest on record and we had no air conditioning, all our matinées played to standing room only.

Now I was really feeling cocky. Again I spoke to Terry, this time proposing that our show be allowed to play the Garrick for a regular run. Terry smiled sweetly and asked, "And what do you suggest we do with *The Guardsman?*" Giving her the benefit of my many years of success in the theatre, I said simply, "Close it." Terry laughed and agreed to discuss the matter with the Guild's board of directors. Within two days I had my answer; *The Guardsman,* which had been running since the previous October, ended its successful run on June 6, and two days later *The Garrick Gaieties* reopened on a regular-run basis.

But not without a few changes. We decided to drop five numbers, including, ironically, "The Joy Spreader," which had been responsible for Larry's doing the show in the first place. Added were "Sentimental Me," a beautiful example of Larry's genius at combining satire and sentiment, a fast-stepping item called "On with the Dance," and a funny sketch by Morrie Ryskind and Phil Loeb based on the Scopes monkey trial. I remember that Lee Strasberg and Harold Clurman played two of the monkeys that made up the jury. To help keep the show fresh, other changes were made in the fall.

Since not all the first-string reviewers had come to see us when we first opened, we were happy to read an almost continuous stream of praise right through to the end of the run, which was late in November. There was even a critical disagreement over Larry's lyrics. Alexander Woollcott wrote in the New York *World* that they were "rich in sprightly elaborate rhymes and suffer only from the not unimportant qualification that they do not sing well." The following day Frank Sullivan answered Woollcott in the same paper. "I liked the lyrics and still do, despite the criticism of a close friend of mine that they are clever but unsingable. I think there is a soupçon of tosh to that argument, although I did not say so in so many words to him. I simply told him he was crazy."

During the run of *The Garrick Gaieties,* those of us who had a hand in the writing were given a small percentage of the gross. I think Larry and I each took home $50 a week, and I also made $83 a week, the union minimum, for the brief period of about a month that I conducted. And finally I had a music publisher. Oddly enough, despite the show's success only one, Edward Marks, showed any interest, and he published seven of our songs. This made a third source of income which, since "Manhattan" managed to catch on so quickly, further contributed to my newly acquired feeling of financial stability.

During June and early July I was living the kind of life I'd always dreamed about. Not only did I have a successful show on Broadway but I was right there every night reveling in it. What's more, I was earning good money and had plenty of time to enjoy myself when I wasn't at the theatre. My parents were spending the summer in Long Beach, so I was free to run around with the kids in the show. Occasionally, on very hot nights, I'd take a late train to Long Beach, where it was always cooler, spend the night at my folks' place, swim or play tennis the next day, and return to New York in time to go to work. Work? It wasn't work. It was my daily encounter with an adoring public, who laughed, clapped, cheered and sent vibrations to the back of my neck. What could be sweeter? Or more unbelievable? Could I really be the same guy who only a couple of months before was ready to go into the babies'-underwear business? Who can tell what would have happened if some kids hadn't wanted to do a revue and if Ben Kaye hadn't thought that his doctor's son was the right man to compose the music?

A few years later Larry and I happened to attend an opening-night performance at the Guild Theatre. Larry looked at the two huge tapestries hanging from the side walls and nudged me. "See those tapestries?" he said. "We're responsible for them."

"No, Larry," I corrected him. "They're responsible for us."

7

In the days when military battles were conducted on foot, it was common practice for the attacking side to keep probing the enemy lines in search of a soft spot. Once the weakness was found, the attacking troops would pour in and fan out. The reception of *The Garrick Gaieties* was the soft spot Larry and I had been looking for, and we were determined to consolidate our gains and make the most of them.

At that time there was a successful comedy on Broadway called *The Butter and Egg Man,* by George S. Kaufman. It was about a prosperous businessman from a small town who comes to New York to invest in plays, and for a while the term "butter-and-egg man" became familiar in theatrical parlance as a substitute for "backer" or "angel."

One morning I got a call from Helen Ford, our once intended star of *Dear Enemy,* who had never lost faith in the show. All she had to say was "I've got the butter-and-egg man," and I knew exactly what she meant. Actually, Robert Jackson was a good deal more than the hick comic figure of the Kaufman play. He owned a chain of stores in Canada, and later became a well-known figure in Washington political circles (not to be confused, however, with the Robert H. Jackson who served as Supreme Court Justice). But the most important thing was that he was stage-struck, and with Helen Ford as our star saleslady, we encountered little difficulty in prying loose the necessary money. After all, Rodgers and Hart were no longer nobodies; we were, if you please, the Theatre Guild's distinguished composer and lyricist who had recently displaced Alfred Lunt and Lynn Fontanne at the Garrick Theatre.

Jackson turned out to be a jolly extrovert, and he had no wish—thank God!—to interfere with us. As soon as we were assured of financial backing, Herb Fields, Larry and I met with Helen and her husband, George Ford, who was her manager. George had run a stock company in Troy, New York (where he and Helen met and married), and was a descendant of the man who had built the famous Ford's Theatre where Lincoln was shot. At Helen's suggestion George became our producer. Even before we began putting together the cast, we decided on the unusual step of previewing the show far from the regular pre-Broadway tryout route. We felt it was necessary because so many people had advised us that a musical dealing with the American Revolution might be commercially risky. But there was another reason why we wanted to test the show as thoroughly as possible before bringing it to Broadway: since Larry and I had achieved our first success with a collection of unrelated songs in a revue, *Dear Enemy* would be our first chance to demonstrate what we could do with a score that had at least some relevance to the mood, characters and situations found in a story. It's tough enough to follow a hit, but we did think it was important to come up with something totally different from what we'd done before. Of course, to do something only because it's different makes about as much sense as following up a hit with something like it only because it's almost the same. Calculation shows through in both cases, and more often than not the results prove self-defeating. Fortunately, with *Dear Enemy* we were able to go back to a show that we'd loved and lived with even before we learned how to spell "Gaieties."

George Ford found a stock company in Akron, Ohio, that was willing to let us use its theatre, the Colonial, and also to provide all the necessary actors to round out the cast supporting Helen Ford. I gave up my conducting chores at the Garrick early in July, and we all journeyed out to Akron. With George's brother, Harry, directing, we rehearsed for only one week, but our opening went well enough considering the fact that there really wasn't enough time to achieve a professional level. From what we saw and from the comments we heard, we were emboldened to go ahead with our plans to mount an elaborate Broadway production. As soon as we returned to New York, we got in touch with John Murray Anderson. We found him just as enthusiastic as before, particularly since we no longer had any problems of financial support, and he agreed to take charge of the overall staging. This meant supervising every aspect of the production, including costumes, scenery and lighting, so that there would be a cohesiveness and style to the show that set it apart from most others of the time.

Rehearsals for this production are less clear in my mind than the first reading of the score at the Knickerbocker Theatre. The orchestration had been done by Emil Gerstenberger, a tough, feisty little man who yelled a lot but never seemed to mean it. During the lunch break, Emil and I left together to get something to eat at a nearby restaurant. Walking down the street, I asked him what he thought of my conducting. "Your ass is in Egypt!" he bellowed. "Stop waving your arms around like a goddamn ballet dancer. You gotta remember to always cut the corners with your beat. Every movement's gotta be so clear that the men know whether you're conducting in four-quarter time or three-quarter time. The girls may think you're cute, but you hafta learn to make every gesture mean something to the musicians." Thereafter, I never forgot to cut the corners.

After deciding to lengthen the title from *Dear Enemy* to *Dearest Enemy,* we played a week in Ford's Theatre in Baltimore, a natural choice considering the familial background of our producer. Although there was plenty of work to be done, the most dramatic incident of the week for me occurred not in the theatre but in a delicatessen across the street. I was having lunch there one day when a gallon can of peaches rolled off the top of a huge icebox just behind me, hit me on the head and knocked me unconscious. When I came to, I managed to make my unsteady way over to the theatre for the afternoon performance, the only occasion I've ever failed to derive any satisfaction from conducting my own music.

The vibrations on the back of my neck were pretty good for this show too. Although it was a bit long, the audience was suitably impressed with the general look of the production, and it was obvious that Anderson's close attention to décor and costumes had made a difference. The audience was also taken with the play's opening scene, in which Helen Ford made a fetching entrance clad in nothing but a barrel (she had been swimming nude in the river, and Charles Purcell, as the young British officer, had stolen her clothes). It was a novel way of introducing the inevitable romantic involvement, and helped establish *Dearest Enemy* as something a little more daring than the customary Broadway product. So did an ensemble number sung by the American girls when they're told that the British are coming. It was called "War Is War," and ended with the then shocking lines: "Hooray, we're going to be compromised!/ War is war!"

One of the many useful experiences I had while working on *Dearest Enemy* was that I became aware of the multiple possibilities there are to vary that most essential of all musical expressions, the love duet. The romantic leads in any musical need a theme or motif, something that's "their" song, which is a universally accepted part of the genre. But such a song must express more than romantic attachment. First of all, it should be written in a fresh, unhackneyed way, both musically and lyrically, and it should be able to fit different situations. The repetition of a song, however, should never be used merely to plug the number in the hope of sending customers dashing to their nearest sheet-music or record store. If a song catches on, fine—every writer loves to have a hit—but it must be part of what is happening onstage. Repetition should be used not merely to drum a song into an audience's collective ear, but to make the relationship between the leading characters more meaningful through music.

In *Dearest Enemy,* the big love duet was "Here in My Arms." It was introduced toward the end of the first act and was first sung by the roguish British officer to the cute little American maid as a light-hearted plea for the girl to fall into his arms. She does, of course, suiting the action to a slight change in the lyric ("Here in *your* arms it's adorable"). In the second act, however, after the officer has been trundled off to prison for the duration of the war, the same song takes on a more plaintive tone as it expresses the emptiness of the girl's life without the man she loves. At the final curtain, the girl stands beneath a fluttering American flag, her soldier returns, and the song assumes a third aspect, revealing that now, with the war over, they will always be in each other's arms.

After a week of rewriting and cutting in Baltimore, *Dearest Enemy* had its New York opening at the Knickerbocker Theatre on September 18. The date is interesting to me principally because of the three other musical productions that had their Broadway premieres within the same seven-day period. Two nights before there had been the much-heralded *No, No, Nanette,* the Vincent Youmans show that had just completed a record-breaking year in Chicago. Three nights later came *The Vagabond King,* the Rudolf Friml operetta that was once supposed to have been written by a couple of unknown kids named Rodgers and Hart. And the next night came *Sunny,* starring Marilyn Miller, with book and lyrics by Otto Harbach and my old friend, Oscar Hammerstein, and a musical score by my idol, Jerome Kern. Thus, between September 16 and 22, 1925, first-nighters could attend openings of shows with music by Youmans, Friml, Kern—and Rodgers. Not that *Dearest Enemy* was in quite the same league as the others, nor has it been revived as frequently, but it did surprisingly well in spite of such illustrious competition.

The newspaper reviewers anointed our show with combinations of approving, if hardly ecstatic, adjectives such as "polite, sentimental and prettily embroidered," "gay, gentle and gracious," "mannerly, melodious, sane and charming" and "singularly tuneful, artistic and agreeable." Larry and I had particular cause for pride in some of the comments, especially Robert Benchley's reference to us as "that God-given team." But it was the summation of Frank Vreeland in the New York *Telegram* that really made us feel that all our years of frustration had been worth it, when he wrote: "We have a glimmering notion that someday they [Fields, Hart and Rodgers] will form the American counterpart of that once-great triumvirate of Bolton, Wodehouse and Kern." Apart from the odd implication that Kern was not an American, the comparison convinced us that what we were trying to achieve was at last being recognized and appreciated.

One evening at the Knickerbocker Theatre I remember particularly well. The Benjamin Feiners, whose son, Ben, was a close friend of mine, were sitting in the first row in the left of the orchestra with their daughter, Dorothy. She was pretty but looked very young, and though I was careful to cut the corners while conducting, I couldn't help showing off for her and her parents. A couple of months later, after I had given up my job as music director, Ben and I had a date to go to the movies to see *The Big Parade,* and I went to pick him up. Andrew Goodman, the son of the founder of

Bergdorf Goodman, was at the Feiners' apartment too, calling for Dorothy to see *Sunny*. Suddenly she appeared in evening dress. Although I had seen her at the theatre only a short time before, she no longer looked like just a young kid; in fact, she looked like the prettiest girl I'd ever seen. For the first time in my life, I knew the feeling that Oscar Hammerstein and I would express many years later in the song "Some Enchanted Evening." Ben and I may have gone to see *The Big Parade* that night, but all I saw on the screen was the bright-eyed, smiling face of Dorothy Feiner.

The opening of *Dearest Enemy* gave me two shows running concurrently on Broadway, a situation that could not have escaped the attention of Max Dreyfus. Sure enough, it wasn't long before I received the royal summons: an invitation to meet with the music publisher in his office. Summons or not, it was one meeting I was looking forward to, particularly in light of my previous unhappy encounters with both Max and his brother, Louis.

As soon as I arrived at T. B. Harms, Inc., the bustling Dreyfus headquarters, I was ceremoniously escorted in to see the great man. Dreyfus rose solemnly from his desk, greeted me warmly and immediately got down to business. Not only did he want to publish the songs from *Dearest Enemy,* he also wanted Larry and me to sign with his company as staff writers. Well, if he didn't remember having once dismissed my efforts as valueless, I certainly wasn't going to bring up the matter at this point. Of course, if my neck had been a bit stiffer than it was, I could have refused the offer, confident that I'd have no trouble finding another publisher. But this was Max Dreyfus, the publisher of Victor Herbert, Jerome Kern, George Gershwin and Vincent Youmans. To have a T. B. Harms label on the songs of Rodgers and Hart was an unequaled sign of prestige. Max Dreyfus may not have been aware that he was eating crow, but that didn't make any difference. Without a moment's hesitation I told him that Larry and I would be glad to accept his offer.

Dreyfus smiled and leaned back in his chair. Peering down his aquiline nose, he said, "There's one thing that puzzles me. Why didn't you ever bring me your songs from *The Garrick Gaieties*?" Attempting to keep calm, I told him that we had tried desperately to get someone from his firm to attend one of the special matinées but that Harms hadn't even bothered to send an office boy. Then, feeling a bit more secure, I told him that "Manhattan," the biggest hit in the *Gaieties,* was one of the songs I had played when Larry Schwab brought me to see him a few years before, and I couldn't help reminding him that he had said there was nothing of value in what he'd heard.

Dreyfus looked slightly stunned, and then quickly changed the subject by explaining the conditions under which writers worked at Harms. He would, he said, be glad to give Larry and me a drawing account similar to that given other staff writers, an offer that made no impression on me, since I didn't have the faintest idea what a drawing account was. Dreyfus explained how it worked: a number of "my boys," as he called them, were permitted to draw anywhere from $50 to $200 a week, and these sums were deducted from royalties when they became due. I suppose something of my grandfather's pride took over at this point because I found myself grandly telling him that Larry and I didn't want to work that way. We wanted nothing in advance, and would be perfectly content to wait until we received all the royalties to which we were entitled.

Dreyfus stared at me with a look of disbelief. "All right," he said, "if that's the way you want it, but I'll tell you one thing. In all my years in the publishing business, this is the first time anyone has ever turned down an advance." Then he put his arm around my shoulder, and I suddenly realized what it meant to be one of Max Dreyfus' boys. "There's one thing I want you to promise me," he said. "If you ever need money, I don't want you to go to anyone else but me. From now on, don't ever forget that I'm your friend."

I never did. Max and I, in fact, remained close friends until the day he died, nearly forty years later. It was a good relationship. Max was a shrewd bargainer and a hard man to get along with, but I never had any trouble with him, nor did he with me. I always felt that I could have gone to him for any reasonable amount of money, but I also knew that when it came to deals involving copyrights he could be really tough. He used to tell me that since he had no kids of his own, his copyrights were his children, and he was going to protect them as carefully as he could.

Max had come to the United States from Germany when he was a boy, and his first job—which I always found hard to imagine—was playing cornet on a Mississippi showboat. A frustrated composer, he gradually worked his way into the music-publishing business, first as an arranger, then as a salesman, and finally as the most powerful publisher in the field. In the late twenties, after reorganizing his firm as Chappell Music, named after the prestigious English firm he had bought, he sold part of the Harms catalogue to Warner Bros. for over $8 million.

Apart from his skill as a businessman, Max had one talent that any musician would envy. He could pick up the orchestra score of a symphony or an opera, settle himself in a comfortable chair and read it the way anyone else would read a novel. He loved to live well, and for a time he and his wife had an elaborate estate in Bronxville, from which they would commute to a large cattle farm in Brewster.

As long as I knew him, Max was always what is generally described as "painfully thin." In his case, however, the adverb was not hyperbolic. Throughout his life there was hardly a time when he was not afflicted with some illness, often a serious one. In the early thirties, shortly after Dorothy and I were married, he was so sick that when we drove up to Bronxville to see him, we fully expected that it would be for the last time. But Max fooled everybody; when he died in 1964 he was in his ninetieth year.

Soon after the opening of *Dearest Enemy* I formed another valued and enduring friendship. I have already mentioned the three other major musicals that opened in the same week as *Dearest Enemy*. In addition, a drama that had its premiere on the very same night as *No, No, Nanette*—September 16, 1925—was to serve as my introduction to one of the theatre's supreme talents.

The play was *The Vortex,* and the author, in his first Broadway appearance, was Noël Coward. A daring study of upper-class decadence, *The Vortex* was a resounding hit, and I was fortunate to get tickets to a Saturday matinée. Though I was impressed with the writing and acting, the high point for me, possibly because it was so unexpected, occurred in a party scene early in the second act. Urged on by his friends, the character Noël was portraying sat down at the piano to play a dance number which turned out to be my own song, "April Fool," from *The Garrick Gaieties.* It was not then, nor has it ever been, well known, and since I was aware that Coward himself was a gifted songwriter, I took it as a tremendous compliment that he would choose "April Fool" over something better-known, or something that he himself had written.

A couple of days later I went to Rudley's, a restaurant in the theatre district, for lunch. Rudley's was below street level, and as I walked down the steps I happened to notice a couple seated at a side table. The man's trim elegance and the slightly Oriental cast to his features could belong to no one else but Noël Coward. We had never met, but I knew that I had to speak to him. Although well aware of his reputation for cutting remarks and the fact that he could devastate my naïve enthusiasm with no more than a raised eyebrow, I boldly walked over and introduced myself. "I'm Dick Rodgers, and—" I began. No sooner did I get the words out than Coward jumped up from his chair, threw his arms around me and proceeded to shower me with praise. Every time I tried to get in a word about how much I admired his play and his music, he would top me with a new expression of admiration for *my* music. When I finally left his table, I was so overcome that I simply walked back up the steps and out of the restaurant. It wasn't until I was halfway down the block that it dawned on me that I hadn't had any lunch.

This sort of enthusiasm for other people's work was typical of Noël Coward, just as his criticism was as outspoken as it was deft. Perhaps his outstanding quality was style. He wrote with style, sang with style, painted with style, and even smoked a cigarette with a style that belonged exclusively to him. Despite his ability to do so many things so superbly, he always had to endure the put-down that anyone so versatile could not possibly be a first-rate talent. What nonsense! Versatility on so high a level needs no excuse. Even one of his lesser-known operettas, *Conversation Piece,* contains more charm, skill and originality than fifty musical plays put together by men specializing in particular fields.

These were cup-runneth-over days for Larry and me. We had written songs for a successful revue, we had proved we could also write a complete score for a book musical, Max Dreyfus was our publisher, and couples were asking dance bands to play "Manhattan" and "Here in My Arms." Recording companies were beginning to record our songs, including a medley from *Dearest Enemy* performed by the Victor Light Opera Company, the nearest thing then to an original-cast album. To top off the year, we were admitted to membership in the American Society of Composers, Authors and Publishers, that impressively titled organization which makes sure that composers and lyricists are compensated whenever their works are performed publicly for profit. Today it isn't hard to join ASCAP, but in those days it was an exclusive outfit, and being accepted as members was further proof that Rodgers and Hart had not only arrived but were considered by their peers to be more than just transients.

Surprisingly, there were few changes in my personal life. I still lived at home with my parents and was still expected to let Mom know if I'd be late for dinner. I honestly felt that the achievements of my brother, who had already begun his medical practice, were far more worthy of praise than mine. My friends were the same neighborhood kids I'd gone around with all of my life. I may have been making more money than ever before, but that wasn't saying much.

Had I come from a very poor family, the change in my life style would probably have been more noticeable. Perhaps I would have lost my head and bought more clothes than I needed, or spent my late hours in those forbidding haunts known as speakeasies. But my family was middle-class, sympathetic and understanding, yet never indulgent, and it simply didn't occur to me to behave differently. My folks had seen me through some miserable times when I certainly couldn't have been a joy to have around the house, and now that things seemed to be working out, it was great fun to share my happiness with them. In fact, my father was the organizer and keeper of my scrapbook, carefully pasting in anything he found in the press about me.

Our newly attained successes also made little difference in Larry's life. Basically he was the same sweet, self-destructive kid I had always known.

A second reason that contributed to my keeping on an even emotional keel was the nature of my work. Though I write the songs and may even conduct them, the audience sees and hears someone else. To paraphrase Oscar Hammerstein, a song becomes a song only when someone sings it. It's the singer up there in the spotlight who gets the applause and who is identified with what is being sung. This is as it should be, but what it can do to a singer's ego is another matter, and it frequently takes an iron will to keep the performer from considering himself the creator.

For example, I'm sure I still recall vividly the thrill of meeting Noël Coward only because my life has not been spent bowing and blowing kisses to my dear public. I enjoy conducting, but that's a purely personal enjoyment. My ego is satisfied merely by hearing my music and knowing that others also derive pleasure from hearing it. I can think of nothing more emotionally satisfying than driving all alone in a car late at night, switching on the radio and listening to one of my songs come at me out of the dark.

Another factor that helped me stay relatively level-headed during those first success-filled months was the precarious nature of the theatre itself. No one has ever had a life in the theatre consisting solely of successes. Anyone entering the field must be conditioned to accept a certain amount of failure; he can only pray that the averages turn out in his favor. At the age of twenty-three I had already painfully learned about failure in my career before *The Garrick Gaieties,* and I knew that my life would not continue forever as blissfully as it was now. No matter how long it runs, every show must have a final curtain, and nothing is to be gained from continuing to savor a success or brood over a flop. When one show is finished, the only thing to do is go on to the next one—and hope.

By the end of 1925 I was already working on the next one—except that it wasn't on Broadway or even in a regular theatre.

As mentioned earlier, the only way we had been able to get *The Melody Man* on Broadway the previous year was when Larry Hart's father hoodwinked Billy Rose into investing $1,000 in that hopeless enterprise. But Billy and Larry had remained friends—partly, I suspect, because Billy, who was still primarily known as a songwriter, needed a handy ghost whenever he got stuck for a lyric. In addition to writing songs, Billy had been operating a speakeasy. But he longed for respectability and felt he could attain status by remodeling a mansion on Fifth Avenue and turning it into a theatre-restaurant. In those days Fifth Avenue was still the site of a number of elegant town houses, and though their owners took a dim view of this commercial invasion, it didn't faze Billy. No liquor was to be served at his Fifth Avenue Club, but customers were assured of getting two things besides food: a steep $5 cover charge and a complete Broadway-type musical revue.

When Billy approached Larry and me to write the songs for the opening show, the idea sounded interesting and we turned out nine or ten numbers. Both the club and the show opened in January 1926, but neither remained open very long. The expected carriage trade found little of attraction in a legitimate, booze-free cabaret, nor was life made any easier by constant complaints from the club's affluent neighbors. Billy sold the place after only a couple of months.

This experience gave me the opportunity to get to know the very shrewd, highly complex and oddly likable character known as Billy Rose. Billy, who was only slightly taller than Larry, was forever churning up new ideas, each more adventurous than the last. Even when one of his schemes fell through, it was never for want of boldness or imagination, nor was it ever from being excessively open-handed. Billy could be pretty tricky, as we discovered when the promised royalties for our revue score failed to arrive. As I recall it, we never collected a dime for our efforts, but Billy was the kind of promoter who somehow made you feel he had paid you double.

Working on the show for the Fifth Avenue Club gave us more time to think about what our next Broadway effort should be. Since we had already written the score for a costume musical, it seemed logical to show what we could do with an up-to-date theme and locale. Six-day bicycle races had recently become a big attraction at Madison Square Garden, and it occurred to Herb Fields that it would make an appropriately topical subject for a musical comedy. He pasted together a plot that was hardly destined to become a classic, but it was lively enough and inconsequential enough to serve the expected function of a musical-comedy book. We called it *The Girl Friend,* after one of the songs in the show.

Most of the songs Larry and I were writing during this period were in the traditional form of song construction at the time. That is, there would be a verse, or lead-in, followed by the refrain, or main body of the song. The verse could be any length, but the refrain was almost invariably limited to thirty-two bars. Construction within the thirty-two bars was also pretty standardized. First there would be a main melodic theme of eight bars, which was then repeated for another eight bars. The third eight—called the "release"—would be a different theme, with the final eight bars returning, often with some variation, to the main theme. This was called the "AABA" form. Another thirty-two-bar form—the "ABAB"—gave equal weight to two melodic themes, though here, too, there might be some variation in the final section. "Thou Swell," which came a bit later, was written in the "ABAB" form. Though occasionally I did play around with the formula —"Manhattan," for example, has no release, or "B" theme, at all—Larry and I never felt restricted but rather enjoyed the challenge of coming up with something fresh within the prescribed regulations.

"Blue Room," which we wrote for *The Girl Friend,* is an interesting example of what I mean. In form it is strictly "AABA," but in writing the main melody, I began the second, third and fourth bars on a C natural— the fifth note of the scale in the key of F—and followed it with a note rising a half tone in each successive bar. This gave Larry the idea of using a triple rhyme on the repeated C note, and then, for emphasis, repeating the word "room" on the rising half tones:

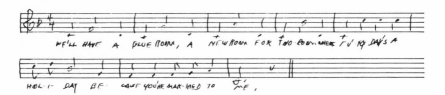

Note how effectively this combination of rhyming and repetition conveys the emotion: "blue room," "new room," "for two room," and then, in the second eight bars, "ballroom," "small room" and "hall room." For the final eight bars, Larry decided against the anticipated repetition and boldly introduced the unexpected references to "trousseau" and "Robinson Crusoe," saving the "blue room" reference until almost the very end of the song. A listener, of course, may not be aware of the technique behind a song, but he is certainly aware of the effect when it turns out right. In "Blue Room" it did.

The Girl Friend brought Rodgers and Hart right back to the man who had given them their start in the professional theatre. Lew Fields had lost money on *The Melody Man* and had been unimpressed with *Dearest Enemy,* but he liked our latest effort and agreed to produce it. For our leads, we had the husband-and-wife team of Sammy White and Eva Puck, two warm, gifted people who had the knack of being funny even when their material wasn't side-splitting. We'd first met Sammy and Eva when they appeared in *The Melody Man,* and they'd impressed us so much that we promised that someday we'd write a show just for them. Unlike most such promises, this one was kept.

*   *   *

When *The Girl Friend* opened in March 1926, it looked as if we were in for our third Broadway success in a row. The first-night audience laughed and applauded with enthusiasm, and most of the reviews were highly favorable. But few things are predictable in show business. Perhaps theatregoers weren't attracted to a story about a six-day bicycle racer; whatever the reason, the show barely limped along for the first week or so, and it looked as if it would have to close. Drastic steps were needed and were taken. Herb, Larry and I agreed to a plan that I think was then unprecedented in the theatre: we offered to suspend our royalties if Lew Fields would keep the show running. Within weeks, word-of-mouth comments and the popularity of the songs "The Girl Friend" and "Blue Room" helped to build our audiences, and soon we were doing great business. *The Girl Friend* played until December, ending up with an even longer run than *Dearest Enemy.* All of which proves that temporary financial sacrifice can sometimes assure eventual financial success. But there are never any guarantees.

During this period I saw a good deal of Lew Fields. Despite that early unhappy experience when he brought in another composer to share the writing of my first Broadway score, our relationship had turned into one of genuine mutual affection. Lew—Mr. Fields to me—was about twenty-five years older than I, and possibly because he had given me my first break, always seemed to have a paternal feeling toward me. He had one habit I used to love. Instead of shaking hands, he would pat me on the cheek, a gesture I found especially endearing since it was so like the kind of thing my grandfather used to do. In all, we were associated in seven Broadway productions, and there was never a single harsh word between us.

At about the time of the opening of *The Girl Friend,* I received a call from Terry Helburn. Since *The Garrick Gaieties* had turned out so profitably, she and Lawrence Langner were all for putting together a second edition, using most of the same people but with all new material. Though we agreed to do it—who could refuse the Theatre Guild?—Larry and I had qualms about the project. The first *Gaieties* had sneaked into town, first as a benefit show, then for a week of matinées, and finally, due to genuine popular demand, for a regular run. What we'd lacked in polish we'd made up for in fledgling enthusiasm, and audiences and critics appreciated the show for what it was. To attempt a similar revue just one year later, it seemed to us, would be extremely risky, for the vital elements of surprise and spontaneity would be hard to recapture. On the other hand, we had no other new project lined up, and we knew it would be fun to be working again with all those talented people. Besides, it was very much in the tradition of the time for popular revues—from the opulent *Ziegfeld Follies* to the intimate *Grand Street Follies*—to spawn successive annual editions.

In the second *Garrick Gaieties* we again kidded the theatre in general and the Theatre Guild in particular, along with other ready-made targets that were fair game for a bunch of smart-aleck city kids. Fully aware that we were sticking our necks out by inviting comparison with the previous *Gaieties,* we tried to disarm the audience by frankly admitting in the opening number:

> We can't be as good as last year,
> For the last year was great.
> How can we compare with the past year?
> It is sad but such is fate.
> We've lost all that artless spirit
> With our Broadway veneer.
> Then it was play
> But we're old hams today,
> So we can't be as good as last year.

Well, we weren't, and critics told us so, but strangely enough, it didn't hurt at the box office. Those who had either seen our show the previous year or who had heard about it couldn't have cared less; *The Garrick Gaieties* was back in town, and that was good enough for them. The second edition ended up running only about a month less than the first.

Two musical numbers from that production are worth mentioning. In the first *Gaieties,* Sterling Holloway and June Cochrane sang "Manhattan"; in the second, Sterling and Bobbie Perkins (June Cochrane was now in *The Girl Friend*) sang a song called "Mountain Greenery." Here, instead of the boy and girl finding the city "a wondrous toy," they decide to leave the city to discover a more romantic setting in the country. The whole attitude was one of urban sophistication amid a rustic atmosphere, which gave Larry a chance to play around with such tricky interior rhyming as "Beans could get no *keener re-/* Ception in a *beanery,/* Bless our mountain *greenery* home." For one of the encores, he even managed to come up with: "You can bet your *life its tone/* Beats a Jascha *Heifetz tone.*"

The other musical number was our first-act finale, "The Rose of Arizona," which, like the previous *Gaieties'* "The Joy Spreader," was a self-contained mini-musical with a book by Herb Fields. Here, for what may have been the first time, a musical revue included a burlesque on the musical theatre itself. We kidded the Kern-Bolton-Wodehouse Princess Theatre shows with a "Till the Clouds Roll By" kind of song called "It May Rain When the Sun Stops Shining" (even ending with "We'll see a sunny day/ For love will find a way/ Till the clouds go rolling by"). We also kidded the heroics of the Friml operettas ("All you Shriners and Elks and Pythian Knights/ And Babbitts of low degree,/ Just listen to me"). Then we had a chorus of flowers sing and dance to the patriotic ode to "The American Beauty Rose," which was full of purposely horrible nonrhymes such as "drizzle" and "Brazil," and "replenish" and "Spanish." "The Rose of Arizona" turned out to be one entry in *Gaieties* No. 2 that most people found superior to its predecessor in *Gaieties* No. 1.

The vigor and originality of the American musical stage during the mid-twenties were much admired, and even envied, by British producers, who began importing Broadway musicals in ever-increasing number. *No, No, Nanette,* in fact, had had a London production even before its New York production, and the Gershwins' *Lady, Be Good!,* starring Fred and Adele Astaire, and *Tip-Toes,* as well as *Sunny,* by Kern, Harbach and Hammerstein, were all reigning favorites. What's more, both Kern and Gershwin had already turned out original scores specifically created for British musicals.

During the winter of 1926, Cicely Courtneidge and Jack Hulbert, a popular English musical-comedy couple, were co-starring in New York in their London success, *By the Way.* It was Hulbert's first time out as producer as well as performer, and while in New York, he and his partner, Paul Murray, spent as much time as possible scouting Broadway musicals for possible importation. Apparently they liked Rodgers and Hart's efforts well enough to get in touch with us, even though stories about the American Revolution and six-day bicycle racing seemed hardly the stuff of which successful West End musicals were made.

Hulbert was an ebullient Englishman with a half-moon smile and an aggressively jutting chin, and Murray was a likable Irishman with a good deal of persuasive charm. Since neither one of our book musicals was deemed appropriate, they came up with the idea that Larry and I write the score for a musical, *Lido Lady,* for which they already had the libretto and in which Hulbert and his wife were planning to appear. This was especially intriguing because Larry and I had recently seen *By the Way* and were very much taken with Cicely Courtneidge's wacky but ladylike clowning. The only problem we could see was that in the musicals we had written with Herb Fields, the three of us had always worked closely together, and we weren't sure we'd feel comfortable outfitting a score to the specifications of an already written libretto. But who were we kidding? The whole enterprise sounded like an exciting adventure, and we were ready to pack our bags that night.

Presently our plans began to enlarge. The show was not expected to begin rehearsals until early fall, and since its locale was the Lido, it was of utmost importance—we kept telling ourselves—that we first repair to Venice to soak up the atmosphere. Another event contributed to our expanding itinerary: on June 8, 1926, at the Ambassador Hotel, my brother married a girl named Ethel Salant. I was best man, and since Morty and I had shared so much during the past couple of years and had become so close, I found the occasion surprisingly emotional.

Suddenly I got an idea. Not only would Larry and I go to Italy, we'd also meet up with Morty and Ethel on their honeymoon. We'd do a little sightseeing, swim in the Adriatic, and end our trip in London writing a show.

What a dull, miserable grind my life was becoming! What could possibly have made me decide against going into the babies'-underwear business?

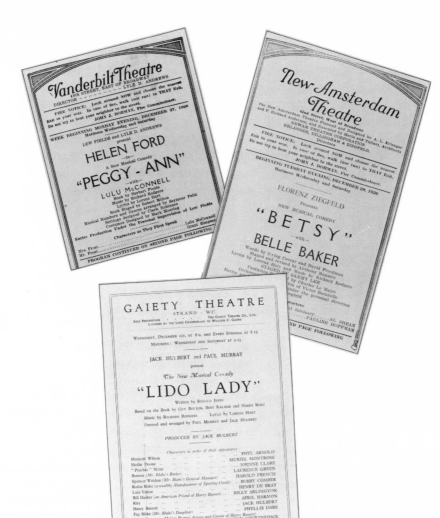

8

Vanderbilt Theatre
48RD STREET, EAST OF BROADWAY
DIRECTOR .... LYLE D. ANDREWS

FIRE NOTICE: Look around NOW and choose the nearest
Exit to your seat. In case of fire, walk (not run) to THAT Exit.
Do not try to beat your neighbor to the street.
JOHN J. DORMAN, Fire Commissioner.

WEEK BEGINNING MONDAY EVENING, DECEMBER 27, 1926
Matinees Wednesday and Saturday

LEW FIELDS and LYLE D. ANDREWS
present

HELEN FORD
in
A New Musical Comedy
"PEGGY-ANN"
—with—
LULU McCONNELL
Book by Herbert Fields
Music by Richard Rodgers
Lyrics by Lorenz Hart
Staged by Robert Milton
Musical Numbers and Dances arranged by Seymour Felix
Settings designed by Clark Robinson
Costumes designed by Mark Mooring
Entire Production Under the Personal Supervision of Lew Fields

Characters as They First Speak ..... Lulu McConnell
..... Grant Simpson
Mrs. Frost .....
Mr. Frost .....

PROGRAM CONTINUED ON SECOND PAGE FOLLOWING

New Amsterdam Theatre
42nd Street, West of Broadway
The New Amsterdam Theatre Planned and Designed by A. L. Erlanger
and P. Richard Anderson, and Executed by Herts and Tallant, Architects
NEWAM THEATRE CORPORATION
ERLANGER, DILLINGHAM & ZIEGFELD
Directors

FIRE NOTICE: Look around NOW and choose the nearest
Exit to your seat. In case of fire, walk (not run) to THAT Exit.
Do not try to beat your neighbor to the street.
JOHN J. DORMAN, Fire Commissioner.

BEGINNING TUESDAY EVENING, DECEMBER 28, 1926
Matinees Wednesday and Saturday

FLORENZ ZIEGFELD
Presents
NEW MUSICAL COMEDY
"BETSY"
—with—
BELLE BAKER
Words by Irving Caesar and David Freedman
Staged and revised by Anthony Maguire
Lyrics by Lorenz Hart and Music by Richard Rodgers
STAGED ..... by SAMMY LEE
Costumes ..... by Charles Le Maire
Orchestra ..... on of Victor Baravalle
Entire ..... under the personal direction
..... Ziegfeld

..... Al SHEAN
..... PAULINE HOFFMAN

ND PAGE FOLLOWING

GAIETY THEATRE
STRAND · W.C.
SOLE PROPRIETOR ..... THE GAIETY THEATRE CO., LTD.
LICENSED BY THE LORD CHAMBERLAIN TO WILLIAM C. GAUNT

WEDNESDAY, DECEMBER 1ST, AT 8.0, AND EVERY EVENING AT 8.15
MATINEES: WEDNESDAY AND SATURDAY AT 2.15

JACK HULBERT and PAUL MURRAY
present
The New Musical Comedy
"LIDO LADY"
Written by RONALD JEANS
Based on the Book by GUY BOLTON, BERT KALMAR and HARRY RUBY
Music by RICHARD RODGERS   Lyrics by LORENZ HART
Devised and arranged by PAUL MURRAY and JACK HULBERT

PRODUCED BY JACK HULBERT

Characters in order of their appearance

Marjorie Wilson	PHYL ARNOLD
Mollie Donne	MURIEL MONTROSE
"Peaches" Stone	JOHNNE CLARE
Benson (Mr. Blake's Butler)	LAURENCE GREEN
Spencer Weldon (Mr. Blake's General Manager)	HAROLD FRENCH
Rufus Blake (a wealthy Manufacturer of Sporting Goods)	BOBBY COMBER
	HENRY DE BRAY
Luis Valero	BILLY ARLINGTON
Bill Harker (an American Friend of Harry Bassett)	APRIL HARMON
Rita	JACK HULBERT
Harry Bassett	PHYLLIS DARE
Fay Blake (Mr. Blake's Daughter)	CICELY COURTNEIDGE
Peggy Bassett (a Motion Picture Actress and Cousin of Harry Bassett)	ROWLAND HILL
Master-at-Arms	

The Gaiety Dancers—DASH FITZGERALD, HARRY WHITE, FRANK TURNBAR, JOE GERALD, and BILLY SHAW
Visitors to the Lido—MARJORIE GENGHISME, MENA BERNARD, BOBBY FRESHFIELDS, NANCY BRO-,
ANN CUTHCOM, CYNTHIA CARLTON, JEAN-ETTE ANDREWS, LILLIAN DU BOIS, LILLIAN LOGAN, VERA
BUTLER, MARY DE POPP, MARGORY DAVIDSON, ERIN BURKE, PAMELA BAXTER, ROSAMUND GARDNER,
ELLA LOWE, RUBIE STEWART, ANNE THURLBY, MARJORIE BELL, MOLLY NEAME, THELMA MORLAND,
VISTA SARANT.
Visitors to the Lido—DENNIS RAY, DONALD AXED, PAUL FRENCH, CHARLES ELLIS, PERCY GALE, GEORGE
GLOSSER, ARTHUR IVES.

As befitted the historic occasion of our first transatlantic crossing, Larry and I chose to make the journey on a ship with the most impressive and musical name we could find. The *Conte Biancamano* may not have been the grandest ship in the Italian fleet but it was roomy and comfortable, and Larry took endless delight in rolling the name around his tongue as if he were speaking Italian. Amid all the hoopla attending ocean trips in those days, we left New York in midsummer. Like most such journeys, ours was both restful and festive. Larry spent most of his time hanging out at the bar when he wasn't hanging over the rail, and I spent most of my time hanging around whatever attractive and unattached girls I could find.

The weather turned balmy as we entered the Mediterranean, and on the night we docked in the Bay of Naples everyone was out on deck to listen to the Italian musicians pouring out such syrupy Neapolitan melodies as "O sole mio" and "Santa Lucia." The music, the star-filled sky and the view of Vesuvius hanging threateningly over the city made the whole scene unforgettable.

But there were even more thrilling sights to come. To get to Bertolini's Palace Hotel, our car had to go halfway up a mountain on the outskirts of the city. Then we had to get out and walk through a tunnel that took us to the center of the mountain, where we boarded a lift that went straight up through rock to the top floor of the hotel. That's where the lobby and the restaurant were located, with the bedrooms below. The view from the top was so breath-taking that even Larry was impressed—at least temporarily.

After spending a couple of days in Naples, we took the wriggling Amalfi Drive down to beautiful Sorrento. But its charms were somewhat ruined for me the morning I awoke and discovered that I had been attacked by an aggressive type of flea that had a nasty habit of burrowing under the skin. From Sorrento we went to Milan, where we had a reunion with my honeymooning brother and his bride. Morty, previously a pretty somber fellow, was practically bubbling; married life obviously suited him.

The automobile drive across the Dolomites to Venice may be one of the most beautiful in the world, but I don't advise it for anyone intimidated by mountain passes. It's a frightening sight to see a bus coming at you on one side of the road and a drop of a thousand feet on the other just as you are rounding a curve with no protective wall. I loved and hated it at the same time, but Larry just hated it. As far as he was concerned, "these mountains are just a lot of rocks."

Venice with its canals, gondolas, St. Mark's Square and Doge's Palace is stamped forever in the mind of anyone who has ever seen a travel folder, but somehow the reality was even more unreal than the image. When one visits Venice, one must of course also visit that luxurious sandbank known as the Lido which separates the city from the Adriatic Sea. One morning Larry and I boarded the public boat that makes the short run from the city to the beach. Seated across the way from us was a woman in her mid-thirties, obviously not Italian. She was blond, slim, patrician-looking without being haughty, coolly oblivious to the heat or the crowd, and I thought she was the most beautiful woman I had ever seen in my life.

As soon as we arrived at the Lido, Larry went in search of the nearest bar and I went for a stroll on the beach. Suddenly I heard a friendly English voice calling my name. To my joy it was Noël Coward, whom I had not seen since our first accidental meeting in the downstairs restaurant in New York. We quickly filled each other in on the reasons why we were there. Noël was in Venice, he told me, visiting an American friend he was sure would love to meet me. We strolled over to his friend's cabana, and I was introduced to a slight, delicate-featured man with soft saucer eyes and a wide, friendly grin. His name was Cole Porter, but at that time neither the name nor the face was in the least familiar to me. However, he was thoroughly familiar with my songs and was almost as effusive in his praise as Noël had been when we had first met. When I told the two of them that Larry Hart was staying with me at a hotel in Venice, Porter insisted that we both join him for dinner that evening at the place he had rented in the city.

Promptly at seven-thirty, Porter's private gondola pulled up outside our hotel. Larry and I got in, were wafted down the Grand Canal and deposited in front of an imposing three-story palace. This was the "place" Porter had rented, which we later found out was the celebrated Palazzo Rezzonico, where Robert Browning had died. We were assisted out of the gondola by a liveried footman wearing white gloves, and ushered up a massive stairway, at the top of which stood Noël, Cole and his wife, Linda. To my happy surprise, she turned out to be the stunning woman I had seen on the boat that morning.

During the delicious and elegantly served dinner Cole kept peppering me with questions about the Broadway musical theatre, revealing a remarkably keen knowledge of both classical and popular music. Since he impressed me as someone who led a thoroughly indolent, though obviously affluent, life, the sharpness of his observations was unexpected. Unquestionably, he was more than a social butterfly.

It wasn't until after dinner, however, that I was to appreciate his remarkable gifts. We went into the music room, where at my host's request I played some of my songs. Then Noël played. And then Cole sat down at the piano. As soon as he touched the keyboard to play "a few of my little things," I became aware that here was not merely a talented dilettante, but a genuinely gifted theatre composer and lyricist. Songs like "Let's Do It," "Let's Misbehave" and "Two Little Babes in the Wood," which I heard that night for the first time, fairly cried out to be heard from a stage. Why, I asked Cole, was he wasting his time? Why wasn't he writing for Broadway? To my embarrassment, he told me that he had already written four musical-comedy scores, three of which had even made it to Broadway. But little had come of them, and he simply preferred living in Europe and performing his songs for the entertainment of his friends. Later he did admit that he hoped someday to be able to have the best of both worlds: working on Broadway and living in Europe. What's more, he said, he had discovered the secret of writing hits. As I breathlessly awaited the magic formula, he leaned over and confided, "I'll write Jewish tunes." I laughed at what I took to be a joke, but not only was Cole dead serious, he eventually did exactly that. Just hum the melody that goes with "Only you beneath the moon and under the sun" from "Night and Day," or any of "Begin the Beguine," or "Love for Sale," or "My Heart Belongs to Daddy," or "I Love Paris." These minor-key melodies are unmistakably eastern Mediterranean. It is surely one of the ironies of the musical theatre that despite the abundance of Jewish composers, the one who has written the most enduring "Jewish" music should be an Episcopalian millionaire who was born on a farm in Peru, Indiana.

That night is still as clear in my mind today as it was then. Though I was unaccustomed to such glittering grandeur, Noël and the Porters turned the occasion into one of the warmest, most relaxed and happiest evenings of my life. Everything else in Venice seemed a letdown after that.

Next stop: Paris. Larry and I took a neck-craning train ride from Venice in high anticipation of the pleasures of life in that fabled city. But Paris was a disappointment. We had no friends there and had to be content with the usual Eiffel Tower–Arc de Triomphe–Louvre–Sacré Coeur sightseeing round. Perhaps it was the weather or perhaps it was just us, but everything seemed drab, and I don't think we saw one smiling face the entire two weeks we were there. Somehow I had the feeling that every Parisian, from taxi driver to head waiter, was trying to take advantage of a couple of innocents abroad. We were reconciled, however, by the prospect that after Paris came England, where we'd be getting back to work and meet all sorts of interesting people who spoke our language.

Our stay in England began promisingly enough. We took the ferry from Calais to Dover and got on the London train in time for tea. Sharing our compartment was a middle-aged, properly tweeded Englishwoman who watched quietly as she saw us struggle over the frustrations of the English monetary system. Apologizing for intruding, she asked if she might be of help. She helped in two ways: first, by spending the rest of the trip to London patiently explaining the British system of pounds, shillings and pence; and secondly, by revealing that, contrary to legend, the English people are not cold and unapproachable. This initial impression has been reinforced almost every time I've had occasion to visit the country.

Of course there are always exceptions found in any such generalization, and it was just our bad luck that the two exceptions we found on our first trip to London happened to be our producers, Messrs. Jack Hulbert and Paul Murray. They had booked us into the Savoy Hotel, but instead of the large rooms with a sweeping view of the Thames that we had been promised, we had to be content with two small dark rooms with no view at all. The Hulberts and the Murrays were well aware that this was our first visit to London and that we didn't know a soul there, but apparently they couldn't have cared less. I recall our having dinner one night at the Murrays' home, but that was the extent of our producers' concern for the composer and lyricist they had specially imported from New York. Since rehearsals were still some weeks off, we had little more to do than write our songs and take in the tourist attractions. There was one difference: unlike Paris, where we were thrown by the language barrier, among other things, we could enjoy the theatre. Not only did we see such transplanted Broadway hits as Gershwin's *Lady, Be Good!,* still starring the Astaires, and *Tip-Toes,* we also had fun at such home-grown entertainments as *Cochran's Revue of 1926* and the long-running *Co-Optimists,* with Stanley Holloway.

Making songs fit into an already written script (some fluff about a flapper tennis champ on the Lido who is pursued by an unathletic suitor) was certainly less stimulating than the give-and-take sessions we were accustomed to having with our old librettist buddy Herb Fields. To make matters even less appealing, we soon found out that the role of the young heroine would be played by an actress who, though unquestionably popular and talented, was pushing forty and looked it. Without much effort we managed to come up with the required number of songs which, "inspired" by our recent sojourn on the Adriatic, included a tune called "Lido Lady" and another called "You're on the Lido Now." Paying due respect to the city in which we were toiling, we also contributed a duet called "A Little

Flat in Soho." And since "Here in My Arms" was unknown in England and could easily be fitted into the story, we dusted off the hit song of *Dearest Enemy* and added it to the new score.

But we were becoming so bored with the project that once we finished the songs, we told Hulbert that if there were no further need of our services we'd be just as happy to pack up and go home. Not surprisingly, no one objected. The London assignment that we had looked forward to with such anticipation had turned so sour that we didn't give a damn whether or not we ever saw *Lido Lady*. What really bothered us was that we never did discover the reason why, after being so friendly and enthusiastic when we first met in New York, Hulbert and Murray had turned so cold and distant in London.

We booked passage on the *Majestic,* the next available ship for New York, and a day or two later we took the boat train for Southampton. The *Majestic* was to make one stop, at Cherbourg, to pick up passengers from France, and printed lists were handed out of the passengers who would soon be coming aboard. I quickly flipped through the list to see if I could find a familiar name. Could I indeed! There, in bold letters, I read:

MR. AND MRS. BENJAMIN FEINER
MISS DOROTHY FEINER

Miss Dorothy Feiner was, of course, that lovely-looking girl I had seen a year before when I called for her brother, Ben. By now she would be old enough to take a long look at, so when we pulled into Cherbourg harbor and the tug with the new passengers came alongside, I was at the rail waiting for her. Even a short look convinced me that I was not going to have a lonely voyage.

Dorothy seemed to be as pleased to see me as I was at the sight of her. The seas were calm and the weather warm, and the two of us spent all our waking hours together, from the morning walks around the promenade deck to the late-at-night sessions on the sun deck. By the time we reached New York we had managed to get to know each other well enough to know that we wanted to know each other better.

As the *Majestic* steamed into New York harbor, the sound of singing and band music sent everyone scurrying to the starboard side of the ship. There, alongside the *Majestic,* was a tugboat with a large banner reading "WELCOME HOME, DICK AND LARRY." Dick and Larry? That's us! Aboard the tug were all the kids from *The Garrick Gaieties* singing the songs from the show and waving to us. It may have been a press agent's gimmick, but it was one hell of a homecoming.

Now that I had got to know Dorothy, I had a special reason to be glad to be home. But having graduated from Horace Mann the previous June, she would soon be leaving for Wellesley, and I would be able to see her only on weekends. With just a week before her departure, we took advantage of the brief time by spending every evening together. She was so bright, so quick-witted and so lovely to look at that I knew then that I would never look anywhere else.

Fortunately, I had plenty to do to keep me from mooning while Dorothy was away at college. Just before Larry and I left for Europe, Herb Fields had discussed with us the possibility of joining him in a highly original concept. Many years before, Lew Fields had produced a musical called *Tillie's Nightmare,* starring a hefty comedienne named Marie Dressler who later became popular in the movies. Herb thought the show could be rewritten and modernized with a new score and a younger, more attractive leading lady. Larry and I liked the idea immediately and began working on it early in the fall. It wasn't hard to sell the show to Lew Fields, and he agreed to produce it with Lyle Andrews, the owner of the Vanderbilt Theatre. Originally we called the show *Peggy,* but by the time it reached Broadway it was renamed *Peggy-Ann.*

Back in 1920 Larry and I had written a song called "You Can't Fool Your Dreams" for *Poor Little Ritz Girl,* which may well have been the first Broadway show tune to have indicated that its lyricist had at least a passing knowledge of the teachings of Dr. Sigmund Freud. By 1926 Freud's theories, though much discussed, had not yet found expression in the theatre, and the time seemed ripe for a musical comedy to make the breakthrough by dealing with subconscious fears and fantasies. That's exactly what we did in *Peggy-Ann.*

To begin with, the entire show, except for a prologue and epilogue, was all a dream. In one scene Peggy-Ann finds herself on board a yacht, where she is to marry the leading man. Her mother, acting as minister, performs the ceremony using a telephone book as a Bible. Peggy-Ann shows up for the occasion in her underwear. After the yacht is wrecked, the wedding party is towed ashore by an enormous fish. They land in Cuba, where Peggy-Ann and her husband go to the races and win the entire island. It was all absurd but meaningful in an avant-garde sort of way. Luckily, the daily critics appreciated what we were doing, and praised us in such terms as "far from the familiar mold," "sprightly and imaginative," "futuristic," "a really bright piece of nonsense" and "far different from the usual pattern."

Working on *Peggy-Ann* was a joy because the whole production was a family affair. In addition to being reunited with Herb and Lew Fields, we were happy, after much delay, to have the leading role played by Helen Ford. Others in the cast were Lulu McConnell, a lovable comic we'd known ever since *Poor Little Ritz Girl*, and Edith Meiser and Betty Starbuck, both of whom had been in *The Garrick Gaieties*. Even the music director, Roy Webb, was the man who had taught me the rudiments of musical notation and conducting during my amateur-show days. The genuine fondness and admiration we all had for one another made it doubly gratifying when *Peggy-Ann* became one of the successes of a season crowded with no fewer than forty-seven new musical comedies and revues. It remained at the Vanderbilt for ten months, and then toured for four.

It is in the nature of things that we live in a balanced world. We expect a certain amount of happiness and a certain amount of unhappiness; we are conditioned to a life in which failure can easily follow success, just as success can easily follow failure. After the coldness of our association with *Lido Lady*, the warmth of our association with *Peggy-Ann* seemed a natural and inevitable antidote. Perhaps it is this element of apparent inevitability that makes us philosophical about the vagaries of life; we can even see a certain justice in them, particularly if the wins exceed the losses. Yet it's hard to think there was anything balanced or inevitable about the mess Larry and I deliberately got ourselves into while we were working on *Peggy-Ann*.

One day Florenz Ziegfeld called. Though Larry and I were now well established on Broadway, as soon as I heard the name Ziegfeld it was like Moses hearing the voice of God on Mount Sinai. Ever since 1907, with his first *Follies*, Ziegfeld had been the acknowledged master producer on Broadway. He was the Great Glorifier, whose shows were the most dazzling and whose stars were the most celestial. The Ziegfeld name on a *Playbill* was an acknowledged guarantee of quality, glamour and success, and so when Florenz Ziegfeld called, Dick Rodgers went running.

In an excessively ornate office I came face to face with a heavyset, gravel-voiced man of authority with a face dominated by a large crooked nose. Ziegfeld lost no time in outlining his idea. He and his millionaire friend and backer Replogle (he was never called anything but Replogle) had just returned from Europe on the same ship with Belle Baker, a tiny woman with a huge voice whose stage appearances until then had been confined to vaudeville houses. Both he and Replogle, Ziegfeld told me, had been "bowled over" by the singer when she performed at a ship's concert, and they were both convinced that she had the makings of a major Broadway attraction. The producer had already commissioned a couple of writers, David Freedman and Irving Caesar, to create an appropriate vehicle, and had even begun lining up a supporting cast. Now, if Larry and I would agree to do the score, the show, which was to be called *Betsy,* would be all set to go into rehearsals in a few weeks.

"A f-few weeks?" I stammered. "We couldn't possibly have it finished in a few weeks. We're already working on a show for Lew Fields."

"I know all about that," Ziegfeld said. "But you two are the whiz kids of Broadway. I'm sure you can do it. Besides"—and here his voice became ever so buddy-buddy—"I wouldn't think of doing it with anyone else but you."

Well, I was only twenty-four and it was the Great Florenz Ziegfeld speaking, and if he felt that way about us, how could I possibly refuse? What a way to end the year—a score for a Ziegfeld production!

I quickly got in touch with Larry, who grumbled a bit but said okay. Apparently even he was impressed by the magic of the Ziegfeld name. When I got home that evening, my parents were surprisingly unenthusiastic. No specific reason, just a feeling. My hunch is that Mom and Pop somehow had the same instinct that makes a lioness apprehensive for its cub. Because *Betsy* turned out to be the worst experience of my career—the worst, that is, until I did another show for Ziegfeld.

During the short period allowed us to create the score, Larry and I seldom saw Freedman or Caesar, and there was hardly any effort at genuine collaboration. I don't think we had more than one meeting with La Belle Baker. Ziegfeld, whose function should have been that of a coordinator, rarely paid any attention to us. There was nothing else for us to do but go our not very merry way trying to write songs that might fit a story for which we had been given little more than a rough outline.

At first I felt rather proud of myself for being able to juggle two scores at the same time. After Dorothy had been at Wellesley for about a month, I wrote her about it:

> I have been doing a terrific amount of manuscript work in the past few days, and I'm delighted with the way my eyes have been behaving. However, it leaves me awfully groggy. There's something like two hours' work on each manuscript and though I have worked hard at it, there are at least twenty-five numbers still to be done. Of course, there are more things to write, and when both shows are seriously in rehearsal I expect to give up eating and sleeping entirely.

By mid-November, with both musicals now scheduled to open on Broadway almost simultaneously the following month, a serious problem had developed with *Peggy-Ann:* we still didn't have a leading lady. Our first choice had been Helen Ford, but she was on the road in *Dearest Enemy*. Then we tried to get Ona Munson, a bright ingénue who had played the title role in *No, No, Nanette* both on tour and in New York, but we let her get away. We held audition after audition, but still couldn't find anyone to play the part.

Within a few days, however, I was able to write Dorothy:

At this particular moment I feel much as though I'd been passed very slowly through a wringer and hadn't been hung out to dry. It's been one of those tough days, with nothing happening badly but everything happening with difficulty.

But as the saying has it, after the R. comes the S. Following two disheartening hours trying to squeeze a glimmer of intelligence from the latest applicant for the part of Peggy, Herb decided to give Helen Ford one more try. We got her on the phone in Cincinnati—and Herb leaves tomorrow night with a contract and a manuscript! It seems *Dearest Enemy* is to close next week and Helen will be Peggy after all! It's been a strain, you see, because we're sure we have a good play to begin with, and we have the best directors there are, and to be forced into such a disagreeable position was rotten. Now I hope everything'll be all right.

In Mr. Ziegfeld's office yesterday morning was assembled all the cast and all the authors and all the directors. The purpose of the meeting was to read the book and play the score. It was a most unpleasant session for me, as I hate to play for friends, much less a bunch of actors whose only thought is exactly what and how much each is to do. However, the book is funny, at any rate, and you realize how important that is. Rehearsals begin definitely today, so we're off! God be with us; it's going to be a terrible siege!

Which, as it turned out, was hardly an overstatement. A week later I wrote:

There was a terrible blowup Friday evening when Z. and his general manager bawled me out for not appearing at enough rehearsals. Z. said some rotten things, and I told him I was through with his lousy show. The general manager also made some cracks and I raised hell.

Yesterday morning Dreyfus sent for said g.m. who came over to Harms to apologize to me. Last night Z. and I were walking around rehearsals with our arms about each other's waists. That's that . . .

My earlier prediction of giving up eating and sleeping while the two shows were in rehearsal was pretty accurate. But I still found time to dash off a letter to Dorothy:

> *Peggy* is such a daring idea and is being done to the limit, while *Betsy* is so much applesauce. I started work early this morning and quit at 12:30 to go out for a sandwich. After 3 o'clock in the afternoon I feel like an old man and act it. I haven't shaved since Wednesday night, and Thanksgiving Day was spent at three different rehearsals . . .

One day early in December, Ziegfeld telephoned to ask Larry and me to join him for dinner that evening at his home in Hastings. Great, I thought; now at last we can really thrash over many of our problems. (Despite his concern for my attendance at rehearsals, Ziegfeld was always too busy to have any time for serious discussions.) He sent his chauffeur-driven Rolls Royce to pick us up—a sure sign of our favored position—and we were greeted at his home by his wife, Billie Burke, who couldn't have been more gracious. We enjoyed a sumptuous meal and the conversation flowed, but every time either Larry or I broached the subject of *Betsy*, our host would always find something else to talk about. After dinner we repaired to the drawing room, where at last Larry and I discovered the reason why we had been so grandly entertained. It seemed that now *we* were obliged to do the entertaining: Ziegfeld simply instructed us to go to the piano and perform all the songs from *Betsy* for the amusement of his nine-year-old daughter.

Betsy was an enormous show with dozens of elaborate scenes, a large cast and hundreds of little chorus girls milling around like mice in an endless stream of "production numbers." It should have been kept on the road for months before being allowed to open in New York; instead, it had just one week at the National Theatre in Washington. During that week panic took over. Freedman and Caesar fought with each other, Larry and I fought with Freedman and Caesar, and Ziegfeld went charging around the theatre, screaming like a wounded water buffalo. After the Washington opening I wrote Dorothy: "I don't like it at all. The book, if you can call it that, is terrible, and the score has been such a source of extreme annoyance that I am anxious only to have it done with."

A fitting climax to this whole sorry episode came opening night in New York. Almost at the last minute, without saying a word to anyone, Ziegfeld bought a song from Irving Berlin and gave it to Belle Baker to sing in the show. Not only did the interpolated number get the biggest hand of the evening at the premiere, but Ziegfeld also had arranged to have a spotlight pick out Berlin, seated in the front row, who rose and took a bow.

My mother, whom I took to the opening with me, was too unsophisticated to understand what Ziegfeld's slippery piece of showmanship meant to me, but Dorothy, who was there with a friend, was outraged.

It really didn't take a trained ear to appreciate that the Berlin contribution, "Blue Skies," was a great piece of songwriting, easily superior to anything Larry and I had written for the production, but at the time I was crushed by having someone else's work interpolated in our score—particularly since Ziegfeld had insisted he wouldn't think of doing the show with anyone else. A few words in advance might have eased our wounded pride, but Ziegfeld could never be accused of having the human touch—at least not where men were concerned. He did show consideration for girls, but even there his overriding ego, or insecurity, would occasionally take over. I recall one night at a *Betsy* rehearsal when, for some minor infraction, he turned on Madeleine Cameron, a featured member of the cast, and blasted her to bits in front of the entire company. Even her hysterical tears failed to stop him. No, Ziegfeld was not a nice man.

Anyway, I got my wish: a Ziegfeld production to end the year. There was some solace in the fact that *Peggy-Ann,* which had opened the night before *Betsy,* was on its way to success, but there was scant balm to the ego in the fact that Rodgers and Hart and Florenz Ziegfeld had ended 1926 with the biggest flop of their respective careers.

Naturally, such a disastrous experience made me take stock of what I was doing and where I was heading. From May 1925 through December 1926, Larry and I had written the scores for six Broadway musicals, one night-club revue, and one musical in London. By today's standards, this was an almost unbelievable body of work within so short a time; yet somehow I had managed to find time to conduct, travel to Europe, and fall in love.

In trying to reassess what we had done, Larry and I discovered, without surprise, that we were most stimulated and did our best work for those assignments that were the most challenging, such as the first *Garrick Gaieties, Dearest Enemy* and *Peggy-Ann.* Of equal importance, we found that we needed to work with people who were not merely professionally competent but also easy to work with. Productions such as *Lido Lady* and *Betsy,* which brought us into contact with indifferent or antagonistic people, resulted in what we both felt were inferior scores. It was obviously foolhardy for us to succumb to the temptations of working in a foreign locale, like London, or for a legendary impresario, like Ziegfeld, if we did not believe in the show we were writing.

By the beginning of 1927, the Rodgers and Hart track record was as solid as anyone else's on Broadway, but to keep it solid we knew that we would have to be particularly careful of our future commitments. Being careful, however, did not mean playing it safe; if anything, it meant being careful not to.

There was no question that *Betsy* had been an emotion-draining experience. What Larry and I needed was to get away and try to relax a bit before deciding on any new projects.

To our amazement, we had been getting word that *Lido Lady,* after receiving moderate notices, had become a sellout in London. This seemed as good a time as any to discover what wonders had been wrought on the show that we had walked out on before the opening. Late in January, we sailed for London to take a look.

Lido Lady was a hit, all right. The packed audience roared with laughter at the antics of Cicely Courtneidge and Jack Hulbert, and there was enthusiastic applause after every number. It was gratifying, of course, but also mystifying. We still didn't think it was much of a show. The book was infantile, the jokes stale, the aging ingénue hadn't gotten any younger, and even the songs didn't strike either Larry or me as anything to boast about. Two days later I tried to explain it in a letter to my girl at Wellesley:

> The show has broken all records for the Gaiety Theatre and is playing to constant capacity. No one can tell us whether it or *Sunny* is the biggest hit in London. For a personal opinion, that's another matter. Were I a stranger paying for my seat I doubt if I'd have a particularly wonderful evening, but I'm not, so what's the difference?

At the end of the letter I added a lonely cry: "Why the devil aren't you here? The fun we could have is simply awful! London is in full swing now and there is so much to do . . ."

Hulbert and Murray were no more hospitable this time than on our first visit, but since we didn't expect anything different, we weren't disappointed. After a few weeks, fully rested, Larry and I were all set to return to New York and face the what-do-we-do-next problem when, unexpectedly, we got a call from Charles B. Cochran. Getting a call from Cochran in London was akin to getting a call from Ziegfeld in New York. "C.B." was acknowledged to be the leading producer of the London stage, and his musicals were famed for their opulence, taste and superb showmanship. What could we lose?

Cochran's office was a wonderfully old-fashioned establishment in Old Bond Street. Physically, the producer was not especially distinguished-looking, but it didn't take long for us to appreciate what a unique person he was. Not only was Cochran a man of obvious great experience and keen judgment, he also knew how to deal with people and put them at their ease. We couldn't have been with him for more than ten minutes before we were chatting as if we'd been friends all our lives.

C.B.'s idea wasn't exactly world-shattering; he simply wanted Larry and me to provide the songs for a new revue he was planning for his theatre, the London Pavilion. Because we still had no plans of our own and there were no pressing reasons to return to New York, we looked at each other and said yes on the spot.

Since it was mid-February and the show wasn't to open until sometime in May, Larry and I took off for Paris, primarily to convince Russell Bennett, who was then living there, to do the orchestrations for the score. Russell, even at that time among the most creative arrangers in the theatre, probably has the most amazing powers of concentration of anyone I've ever known. When he eventually joined us in London, I remember walking into his flat one morning to discover him working diligently on the score while listening to music blaring from a radio.

Another reason why we went to Paris was to see if we might not have misjudged it the first time we were there. Somehow, this time the French seemed more friendly, or perhaps it was just that we were getting used to the Parisian way of life. What made our stay doubly enjoyable was that we ran into two girls we had known in New York. With Rita Hayden and Ruth Warner, we made a happy foursome taking in all the expected sights—and a few unexpected ones, too.

While we were escorting the girls back to their hotel one night in a taxi, another cab darted out of a side street and missed hitting us by a matter of inches. As our cab came to a halt, one of the girls cried, "Oh, my heart stood still!" No sooner were the words out than Larry casually said, "Say, that would make a great title for a song." I told him that he was a crazy fool to be thinking of song titles at such a time, but I guess I'm a crazy fool too, because I couldn't get the title out of my head. When the cab stopped at the girls' hotel, I took out a little black address book and scribbled the words "My Heart Stood Still."

After Paris, Larry and I went to the south of France for a few days, but I couldn't help thinking about my freshman in Massachusetts. I wrote Dorothy from Cannes:

> Just before we left Paris there were three letters in a bunch from you. You see, you are every bit as nice as I said you were. And how I enjoyed them! *En passant,* why don't you get yourself fired out of school for smoking! That would settle your problems so well.
>
> Anyway, one helluva good time was had in Paris. We tore the old

place wide apart in a nice way with no ill effects. There were ten days of nearly complete joy. The "nearly" means you, because we could have had fun. No? . . .

When we returned to London, Louis Dreyfus, Max's brother and the head of Harms's London office, suggested that if we were going to stay awhile in the city, we should rent a "service flat" rather than stay in a hotel. A service flat, we quickly learned, was like an apartment except that all the services, including housekeeping and the preparation and serving of meals, were taken care of by the management. The place that Louis told us about was beautifully located, at 29 St. James's Street, between Piccadilly and St. James's Palace. Actually, Larry and I had separate flats on the same floor, with mine conveniently equipped with its own piano. "Here am I back in London at work," a letter to Dorothy announced, "which consists of getting up late, going to rehearsal and making a few pithy suggestions, having dinner somewhere or other, and 'going out.' I'm full of sympathy for myself and don't see how I can stand it."

Cochran's new revue was to be called *One Dam Thing After Another.* Even without the *n* in "Dam," this struck Larry and me as a racy title for an English revue. Others apparently thought so too, since the show was usually referred to as *The London Pavilion Revue.*

While in London, Larry and I went to see another musical, *Lady Luck,* which included two of our songs from *Betsy,* "Sing" and "If I Were You." Opening the program, we read our credit line, "Additional numbers by Rogers and Hart." Even today my name is frequently misspelled, but it no longer bothers me as it once did. (Though it still bothers my wife!) In the mid-twenties, however, whenever I saw a newspaper piece about me in which the *d* was left out of "Rodgers," I was ready to shoot the editor. One day, after having seen my name misspelled in three different articles, I told my father that the only course left was to give up the struggle, admit defeat and drop the *d* myself. Pop bristled slightly, but as usual he didn't give me a flat answer. He thought for a bit, then said, "I'll tell you what: you just make the name so well known that the accepted way to spell it will be with a *d.*" I knew I couldn't win that argument.

Larry and I spent a lot of time working in our adjoining flats in St. James's Street. It was enjoyable, chiefly because Cochran was so encouraging and appreciative of everything we did. He lined up an impressive cast for his revue, including, in her first major part, a very young, bright-eyed and toothy doll of a girl named Jessie Matthews. Also in the cast was Edythe Baker, a brilliant American pianist, whose trademark was a large white piano. A second pianist, for the pit, was Leslie Hutchinson, an extremely personable black man known as "Hutch." He used to appear at all the society parties and was so popular that it was a real coup to have him play in the theatre orchestra.

One morning in my flat I was looking for a telephone number in my address book and came across the words "My Heart Stood Still." Now what the devil could that mean? Then I remembered that night in Paris. It was early and Larry was still asleep, so I simply sat down at the piano and wrote a melody that seemed to express the feeling of one so emotionally moved that his heart has stopped beating. Later, when Larry came in, I grandly announced, "Well, I've set that title to music."

"What title?" Larry asked.

" 'My Heart Stood Still.' "

"Say, that's a great title. Where did you get it?"

He had completely forgotten the taxi incident, but after I played the tune for him he finished the lyric in no time at all. In my entire career this is the only time I can recall in which a specific, totally unrelated incident triggered the creation of one of my songs.

More important than its genesis, of course, is the song itself and the way it illustrates a facet of Larry's talent that has often been overlooked. His ability to write cleverly and to come up with unexpected, polysyllabic rhymes was something of a trademark, but he also had the even rarer ability to write with utmost simplicity and deep emotion. Just look at the lyric to "My Heart Stood Still." With the exception of six two-syllable words, every word in the refrain is monosyllabic. But how direct and affecting it all is with, for example, its tender reference to "that unfelt clasp of hand" and its beautifully contrasting conclusion:

> I never lived at all
> Until the thrill
> Of that moment when
> My heart stood still.

With lovely Jessie Matthews singing it in *One Dam Thing After Another* and Edythe Baker playing it on the piano, this song easily turned out to be the hit of the show.

It will not have escaped the reader's notice that this stay in London was far more enjoyable than the first. The man most responsible for this was unquestionably Cochran, who entertained us frequently in his home and who went out of his way to introduce us to many interesting people. Cochran himself was an admirable blend of gentleness, intellect and courage. His interests were catholic. He brought Russian ballet to England, promoted championship prize fighting, sponsored concerts and produced everything from the heaviest dramas to the lightest musicals. He was a lovely man and I was deeply fond of him.

It was at Cochran's home that I first met Edythe Baker, who was popular with a fascinating segment of London society. Her steady beau, whom she eventually married, was Gerard "Pops" d'Erlanger, the son of Baron Emile and Baroness Catherine d'Erlanger. All the d'Erlangers were great lovers of the arts, including Pops's brother, Robin, and Robin's vivacious wife, Myrtle. Since Larry had discovered his own group of friends, I spent a good deal of my free time with the always exciting and stimulating d'Erlanger clan. Myrtle, in particular, threw some of the gayest parties I've ever been to. Even after her divorce from Robin—when she was given the title, definitive article and all, of "The Mrs. Farquharson of Invercauld"— our friendship continued, until her death during World War II. Today I am still close to the d'Erlanger family through Zoë, Myrtle's daughter, and Zoë's children.

I first got to know the Prince of Wales at Myrtle and Robin's home. He loved all kinds of music, but especially that of the American theatre, and Edythe and I enjoyed playing for him. Because of his friendship with Edythe, the Prince came to the opening night of *One Dam Thing After Another.* I was all agog over this, not only because I was pleased at his being at the show but because I was sure that the resulting publicity would be of tremendous box-office value. Cochran, however, wise to the ways of London audiences, warned me that it could spell disaster, since, given the choice, Britons much preferred spending an evening watching royalty than what occurred onstage.

As the show progressed, it looked as if C.B. was absolutely right. No matter what was happening in the revue, everyone was staring at the royal box, as if to await a signal indicating when to laugh and when to applaud. The Prince was obviously enjoying himself, but by the time the people in the stalls and the circles got the message, they reacted in all the wrong places.

During the intermission Larry and I mingled with the crowd in the lobby, where we overheard two properly starched ladies discussing one of our songs. "That was certainly a hot tune," said one dowager. "Oh, no," corrected her friend. "Mr. Rodgers does the tunes. Mr. Hart does the lyrics." A little later a bejeweled *grande dame,* on meeting Larry, said ever so sweetly, "It's funny, Mr. Hart. It's very amusing. But I don't like funny shows. I like pretty shows."

After the final curtain fell to no more than perfunctory applause, Larry and I went backstage to see Cochran. "Well, boys," he said matter-of-factly,

"I don't know whether to try to make this thing run or close it now and book a film into the theatre." Then the three of us went to his office to have a drink and discuss the show's fate. Neither Larry nor I could offer concrete advice, since we knew next to nothing about London theatre management, but C.B. did agree to keep the show going for a while. Surprisingly, the reviews turned out to be extremely encouraging, and helped the show remain alive until an unexpected piece of luck came our way.

Larry and I had already returned to New York when, three weeks after the show's opening, we received a bundle of newspaper clippings. Though the Prince of Wales had inadvertently almost killed our show on opening night by his mere presence, he now became the one most responsible for turning it into a success. According to the newspaper accounts, he had gone to a dance in Plymouth at the Royal Western Yacht Club and had asked the orchestra leader to play "My Heart Stood Still." Teddy Brown, the leader, didn't know the tune, nor did any of his men, but that didn't stop the Prince. Since he had heard Edythe and me sing and play the number many times, he knew it well enough to hum the melody until the musicians were sufficiently familiar with it to play it. One newspaper, the London *Evening News,* had a big headline blazoning THE PRINCE "DICTATES" A FOX-TROT. Underneath was a subhead, THE SONG THE PRINCE LIKED, and underneath *that* were the printed words and music of the first sixteen bars of "My Heart Stood Still." This royal seal of approval was enough to send Londoners queuing up at the Pavilion box office and scurrying to music stores to buy the sheet music and recordings of the song. Thanks to the Prince of Wales, our revue ran for seven months and Cochran was never forced to book that film.

Our Cochran revue had given Larry and me a breather from the inevitable decision we had to make about our next Broadway show. On returning to New York, we knew we could not postpone it any longer. One thing was certain: it would have to be different from anything we'd ever done before. Apart from our own inclination to try something new, we were well aware of the number of producers and writers who, having had one hit, simply tried to duplicate the formula the next time out—or even worse, tried to copy someone else's formula. Rarely, if ever, did these imitative productions succeed in being anything more than hand-me-down products.

Indeed, there was an appalling monotony of subject matter in even the best musical shows of the twenties. The themes seemed to be built almost entirely around the boy's pursuit of the girl, their breakup in time for the first-act finale (you gotta make the customers want to come back to see how it all turns out), and the eventual reconciliation. There were plenty of variations on the Montague-Capulet theme or the Cinderella—or its variant, the Pygmalion—theme, in which the poor girl ends up beautiful, rich and the Queen of the *Follies*. And there was always the one about the poor girl chasing the rich boy or vice versa—until they both turn out to be either rich and happy or poor and happy. The important thing was that everyone had to end up happy so that the people who bought tickets would leave the theatre happy.

There was essentially nothing wrong with this except that it kept the musical theatre within a structurally uncreative bind. As a composer I should not have been too concerned about this. The simpler and more predictable the story, it might be argued, the more ready the audience is to appreciate the music. If the plot is especially fresh or daring, the theory goes, the composer risks audience resentment at the intrusion of his songs. But this seemed to me both nonsensical and self-defeating. I have always believed that the story and the music must be closely interrelated, and that each component should be strong enough to help the other and contribute to the overall effect. Why should songs rescue a juvenile, hackneyed story? Or even, though less likely, an intelligent, adult story save a weak score? Why can't they both be equally bright, original and enjoyable? I'm not claiming that I was alone in my view. All the major composers of the twenties—such as Kern, Gershwin and Youmans—were constantly seeking ways to break out of the conventional musical-comedy mold, though they often had to write for formula entertainments.

That's why it was always so much fun to work with Larry and Herb Fields. We all liked and respected one another and what each one of us was contributing. After our London sojourn, it was almost inevitable that Larry and I would do our next Broadway show with Herb, and when we got together again to toss around ideas it was also almost inevitable that we would think only of the most challenging and intriguing subjects we could find. This led directly to *A Connecticut Yankee*.

Back in 1921 Larry, Herb and I had seen a moving picture adapted from Mark Twain's *A Connecticut Yankee in King Arthur's Court*. We all thought the story wonderfully funny, with an irresistible combination of fantasy and social commentary, and were sure it had the makings of a first-rate musical comedy. At the time making a musical comedy out of an accepted literary classic may not have been frowned on by producers, but it wasn't exactly encouraged either. But we liked it and wanted to do it; it was as simple as that.

Well, not quite. Charles Tressler Lark, a flinty-eyed character, was the lawyer for the Mark Twain estate. When I first outlined to him our plans to turn the story into a stage musical, Mr. Lark agreed, to my amazement, to let us have the rights without payment. But that was in 1921, when Larry,

Herb and I were still unknown and unable to get a hearing. By 1927 our option on the book had lapsed and when we tried to pick it up again, Mr. Lark, well aware of our successes, made sure that the estate would receive both a high fee and a whopping royalty arrangement.

As the producer who had sponsored most of our past musicals, Lew Fields was our obvious choice to present *A Connecticut Yankee* (the slightly shortened title that we used), and in the summer of 1927 we gave him the Mark Twain novel to read while he was in London directing the English version of *Peggy-Ann.* Surprisingly, he cabled back that he could see nothing in the book that would make a good musical. Still confident that we would have little trouble finding a producer once the script and songs were finished, we went ahead with the project anyway. What Herb Fields did primarily was to update the modern part of the story and use the dream flashback in Camelot as a means to introduce anachronistic humor involving current slang and business technology at the court of King Arthur.

After Lew Fields returned to New York and read what we'd written, he became as enthusiastic as we were and agreed to produce the show. In order to get the Vanderbilt Theatre, where we had thrived with *The Girl Friend* and *Peggy-Ann,* Fields again went into partnership with Lyle D. Andrews, the theatre's owner, who put up a good deal of the capital.

At about the same time, early September of 1927, we were approached by Charles Dillingham, one of Broadway's most respected producers, to write the score for a musical comedy to star Beatrice Lillie. Both Dillingham and Miss Lillie knew of the hit that "My Heart Stood Still" had made in London, and as soon as we had agreed to do their show they both told us how anxious they were for Bea to introduce it to Broadway. Now, Larry and I were well aware that Bea Lillie was a great attraction and a great clown, but we also knew that she simply didn't have the voice to introduce "My Heart Stood Still" to anyone. To get her off our backs, we simply told her that she couldn't have the song because it was already slated for *A Connecticut Yankee.* Of course, once we used the excuse, we had to make sure that the song really was in the show. This meant getting permission from Cochran, since it was still being sung in his revue. He agreed, but only on the condition that Larry and I accept a cut in show royalties. Thus, we found ourselves paying for the right to use our own song, though I have to admit that it turned out to our ultimate advantage.

To play the title role in *A Connecticut Yankee,* we chose William Gaxton, a restlessly dynamic performer, well known in vaudeville but still untried in a Broadway book musical. Constance Carpenter, the love interest, was an English actress who had appeared in the Gershwin musical *Oh, Kay!* the previous season. And directing our dances was an imaginative young man with limited Broadway experience who answered to the highly unlikely name of Busby Berkeley.

Rehearsals were fun, as most rehearsals are, and everyone seemed optimistic about the show's chances. Because of the title, we decided to open out of town in Stamford, Connecticut, but the production was still so ragged that the citizens of the Nutmeg State could hardly have considered it much of an honor. The only really enjoyable part of our stay in Stamford was that Dorothy came down from Wellesley for the opening. She did her best to like the show, but I knew she was being kind. By the time we got to Philadelphia, however, we were in good shape, and we played there for four weeks to sellout business. We did have one major disagreement, which was over the song "Thou Swell"; Lew Fields wanted it cut out of the score. While it is often necessary to remove a particular number if it is inappropriate or slows down the action, in this case there seemed to be no sound reason for dropping the song, and I simply refused to allow it.

Our conductor for *A Connecticut Yankee,* as he had been for *Peggy-Ann,* was my close friend Roy Webb, and because of my confidence in the song and the show, I asked his permission to conduct the first-night performance in New York. On opening night I climbed into the pit, received a polite greeting and led the musicians through the overture. Instead of opening directly into the first act, we began with a prologue in order to separate the show's real world from its dream world. The scene, set in a hotel ballroom in modern-day Hartford, contained two songs, the second being "My Heart Stood Still." Here, I was certain, we would really grab them. To my dismay, however, the song, while greeted cordially enough, didn't produce the enthusiastic reception I had expected. Oh, well, on to Act One. It was here that we began the dream sequence in which Billy Gaxton, having been hit on the head in the prologue, dreams that he is back in the days of King Arthur. In the first scene, the road to Camelot, he meets the fair Connie Carpenter, and after a few words of who-hit-me–where-am-I banter he begins singing "Thou Swell." Billy wasn't more than eight bars into the refrain when I began to feel that something on the back of my neck. It wasn't the steady, growing sensation I'd felt during the first *Garrick Gaieties,* nor was it the more subdued, all-is-well feeling I had during *Dearest Enemy.* This time the audience reaction was so strong that it was like an actual blow. Though there were no audible sounds, I could feel the people loving Gaxton, adoring Carpenter and going wild over the song. The applause at the end of the number was deafening, and Billy and Connie returned to give several encores. That did it; from then on, the show was in. Nothing, I knew, could stop it from being a smash.

After the final curtain there was a genuine ovation, and most of the company went next door to The Tavern, a popular theatrical restaurant, to await the critical verdict in the morning papers. Though there were some reservations about the book, all the reviewers confirmed my feeling that we had a major hit. Brooks Atkinson, in the *Times,* liked everything about it, and gave my music as enthusiastic a review as it has ever received. I have enough company in my affection for Brooks to lead me to believe that this review was not the only justification for my feeling that he was the best critic the American theatre has ever had. Gilbert W. Gabriel, in the *Sun,* was also unreservedly enthusiastic, but it was not until years later, when we became good friends, that I realized that he was the only theatre critic writing for the New York press who had a musician's knowledge of music. I also got a kick out of the notice written by Frank Vreeland of the *Telegram.* Taking his cue from "The Sandwich Men" number in the show, he penned his own sign:

> GO, THOU SLUGGARD,
> AND ENJOY
> "A CONNECTICUT YANKEE"
> AND TELL
> YE COCKE-EYED WORLDE
> THOU HAST HAD
> YE HELLUVA TIME

The success of *A Connecticut Yankee*—the biggest one Larry and I had during the twenties—further confirmed my feeling that taking chances was the only safe thing to do. Unfortunately, however, I was not always able to adhere to this conviction. Being human, I could still be persuaded to take assignments that, if looked at with more objectivity, I should have refused. *She's My Baby* was just such a project.

In 1927 Ziegfeld's only possible rival in America in fame and prestige was Charles Bancroft Dillingham, and Larry and I were eager to write the songs for his new Beatrice Lillie production. Dillingham's office was just above the entrance to the Globe Theatre, which he owned. Oddly enough, I had never met him before, nor did I have any idea of what he looked like. Expecting to meet another rough-and-tough Broadway producer, I was surprised to be greeted by a tall, courtly, neatly mustached gentleman who treated me as if I were doing him the greatest honor merely by visiting him. Briefly, he outlined his plans for *She's My Baby*. He was confident that he'd found an ideal vehicle for madcap Bea Lillie in a farce devised by Guy

Bolton and the team of Bert Kalmar and Harry Ruby, who were considerably better known as songwriters than as librettists.

Since I had long admired Bolton, I was particularly anxious to work with him, and knowing and liking both Kalmar and Ruby was another factor in persuading me to join the new venture. Though the story they had devised didn't strike me as being a world-beater, I felt that Larry and I would not only have fun working with these people but could also learn something from them. And who could resist the temptation of writing songs for Beatrice Lillie, whose irrepressible antics had made her a great favorite in New York ever since *Charlot's Revue of 1924*?

Soon after the successful launching of *A Connecticut Yankee* early in November, we began working on *She's My Baby*. We had already surmounted the first hurdle by keeping "My Heart Stood Still" away from Bea and putting it in *A Connecticut Yankee*. Our second hurdle had nothing to do with the show or the score: it was me. About halfway through the job I got a severe case of flu and had to be bedridden for a couple of weeks. With rehearsals almost ready to begin, I managed to get out of bed and totter down to see Dillingham. He took one look at me and said, "You look terrible. Pack a bag and go down to Atlantic City. Stay there for four or five days and don't do a thing. And remember, you're my guest during the entire time."

That was the kind of man Dillingham was—generous, considerate, always more concerned about people than about business. The kind of man I was? I was a nut. I told him no thanks, that I'd been holding things up long enough and felt that I had to stay home and finish my work as quickly as possible. And I did.

As a producer, Charles Dillingham was tremendously prolific, with an impressive career of over fifty shows, including such hits as *The Red Mill*, *Watch Your Step* and *Sunny*. Yet I found him an enigma as far as our musical production was concerned. Once we'd all signed our contracts, he immediately lost interest in the project. I remember that we had a run-through in Washington, with a dress rehearsal the following night. At the end of the first act of the dress rehearsal, I saw him calmly strolling out of the theatre. "Mr. Dillingham," I called out after him, "what about the second act?" Without breaking stride, he said, "Oh, I saw it last night. I don't have to see it again." I'm sure he must have been at the New York opening, but I can't recall seeing him there or ever hearing another word from him about the show or the score.

In addition to Bea Lillie, *She's My Baby* had an interesting cast. The ingénue was played by Irene Dunne, whose voice and beauty were then just beginning to be appreciated. Clifton Webb, who played a sort of comic romantic lead opposite Bea, was little different from his later Hollywood image—suave, soigné and unflappable. And there was Jack Whiting, whose wavy red hair and ear-to-ear smile made him the epitome of the Broadway juvenile.

She's My Baby, which opened early in January 1928, received only tepid notices, with most of the blame going to the book and most of the praise going to Bea Lillie. Probably because the better songs were written as specialty numbers for Bea, Larry and I didn't come up with anything that lasted beyond the show's two-month run in New York.

So it was another setback for Rodgers and Hart. Not that the experience was in a class with *Betsy.* There were no fights and no bitterness on anyone's part. No one was to blame except myself for having become involved in a show I should have avoided.

During my siege of influenza I had received especially loving care at the hands of both my parents. Pop, of course, was my doctor, but Mom never left the apartment until I was well again. Primarily to show my appreciation for their kindness, I decided to treat them to a trip to Europe. The winter of 1928 was particularly cold and miserable in New York, and with nothing pressing at the moment, I managed to persuade them to take a vacation in Paris and the warm, balmy south of France. A week after the opening of *She's My Baby,* the three of us sailed on the *Columbus,* and were welcomed in Paris by the worst snowstorm the city had had in years. After a day or two of being confined to our hotel, we decided we'd had enough and took off for the Riviera. There was no snow there, but the weather was freezing and the clouds were ominously gray. We weren't licked yet! With stubborn determination we reasoned that all we had to do was to go a bit farther south, to North Africa, where surely we would find a tropical paradise.

We sailed for Algiers on a crowded, filthy little tub with the grand name of *La Moricière.* The crossing was rough, the food almost inedible, and the sole privilege enjoyed by the family Rodgers was sharing the only private bathroom on the ship. We found Algiers fascinating, but only for a day or so. Then the weather turned cold and wet, and once more we found ourselves unable to leave our hotel. Were we depressed? Damn right. Were we defeated? Not on your life. So determined were we to have our elusive, fun-filled holiday in the sun that we hired a car, a big Renault, and a good French chauffeur-guide to drive us over the Atlas Mountains to Setif, on the edge of the Sahara. We drove through the mountains and spent the second night of the trip in a hotel at Constantine. Up early the next morning for the final leg of what had become something of a holy mission, we discovered that the car had broken down and wouldn't budge. Lesser men might have given up right then, convinced that fate had decreed that they would be forever frustrated in their quest for a little warmth and sun. But not the undaunted Rodgerses! We simply hired the only taxi in Constantine to drive us the remaining distance to Setif, and there, at last, we found what we had been searching for ever since we left New York—a bright-blue sky and a warm, sunny climate.

The only trouble was that it had taken us almost a month. Since I was now needed in New York to begin work on a new show, we could enjoy our discovery for only a single day before heading back. Still, we could say "Mission accomplished," and with pride in our fortitude, we took a train back to Algiers, the *Roma* across the Mediterranean to France, and the *Olympic* from Le Havre to New York.

It must have been about five o'clock in the morning when we reached the mouth of the Hudson. Something awakened me, probably tugboats, and I looked out the porthole. There were huge chunks of ice on the Hudson, so the weather was obviously no warmer than when we had left, but the sky was unusually clear and the stars looked as if all I had to do was reach up and touch them. I dressed quickly and ran up on deck to see the breathtaking Manhattan skyline illuminated in the brilliant early-morning glow. As we passed street after street on our way up the river to our pier, I felt the exhilaration of a prisoner about to be set free. The freezing weather bothered me not at all; all I cared about was that I'd soon be home again, seeing Dorothy again and doing the work I loved again.

Larry and I never had any kind of agreement, either written or verbal. Even a handshake would probably have seemed too formal. We simply knew that as long as we both could do the work we did, we would always remain partners.

Our relationship with Herb Fields was much looser. Although, curiously, Herb never seemed to have any great love for the theatre, he was easy to get along with and was always full of ideas, and we enjoyed working with him more than with any other librettist. But none of us ever thought of ourselves as part of an indissoluble trio, even though, up to 1927, Herb had never written with any other songwriters. Early that year, however, before we began working on *A Connecticut Yankee*, he had accepted an offer to join another team, Clifford Grey, Leo Robin and Vincent Youmans. His first effort without Rodgers and Hart turned out to be considerably more successful than any of our early book shows without him, since *Hit the Deck* was one of the decade's most memorable productions.

Having done so well with a musical comedy about the U.S. Navy, Herb began dreaming up an idea to involve another branch of the service, the United States Marines, and this time he brought it to us.

The show was called *Present Arms*. Because we were concerned about a musical dealing with Marines coming on the heels of one dealing with sailors, we did what we could to make the new show as different as possible. Instead of taking our servicemen to China, as in *Hit the Deck*, we took them to Pearl Harbor. Instead of having our heroine chase our hero, we had our hero chase our heroine, and instead of making her a New England seamstress, we made her a titled English lady. Try as we did, though, it all came out as a variation on *Hit the Deck*. This resemblance was reinforced by a particularly short-sighted bit of casting. To play our Marine hero we chose a round-faced, breezy song-and-dance man named Charles King who had just finished playing the sailor hero in *Hit the Deck*.

At the time we went into rehearsals, however, this did not bother us because we were more concerned with other members of the cast. As I wrote to Dorothy about a week before we opened out of town: "The show is quite a problem. We're rather sure, for us, of the book and the score, but the cast remains an unknown quantity. Charlie King looks great, but we don't know about the leading lady, a sweet-looking little English blonde named Flora Le Breton. She does everything well, but she seems to have for most of us the same attraction as a small canary . . .."

Our dance director for *Present Arms*, as for *A Connecticut Yankee*, was Busby Berkeley. This time, however, he wasn't satisfied with just directing the dances; he also tried out for, and got, the second male lead in the show. What may surprise some people today is that it was Busby who, with a juicy little grape of a girl named Joyce Barbour, introduced the musical's most popular song, "You Took Advantage of Me."

This brings up one of the eternal mysteries of the musical theatre. Despite good reviews, it is often next to impossible to predict whether or not a show will be a commercial success. We first learned this with *The Girl Friend*, which got rave notices and almost closed in a couple of weeks. But one might think that predicting a song hit would be easier. Anyone knows that all that is needed is to keep plugging away until the public is so saturated with a number that it is sure to love it forever. But the fact is that no amount of plugging can make people like something they don't respond to, though there are certain songs that, with a little extra help, can achieve popularity. We had hopes for "You Took Advantage of Me," but we had even greater expectations for the more romantic duet, a sweet, charming, tender and eminently appealing ballad called "Do I Hear You Saying, 'I Love You'?" Consequently, we made sure that it was generously reprised throughout *Present Arms*. It was sung in the first scene and in the third scene, it was played during intermission, it was part of the finale, and it was the last music the audience heard as it filed out of the theatre. But people forgot it as soon as they reached the sidewalk. Maybe the title was too long, maybe the music was too delicate, maybe maybe maybe . . . As it turned out, the number everyone did remember—and still does today—was the sassy, unregretful "You Took Advantage of Me."

Since *Present Arms* was about the Marines, we were in agreement that the show would be different in at least one respect from most musical comedies: there would be no effeminate young men in the chorus. We ended up with the toughest, burliest-looking group of singers and dancers ever seen onstage. This turned out to be a mixed blessing when we got to Wilmington for the out-of-town tryout. What we hadn't counted on was that our Marines not only looked like real Marines, they also tried to act like them. Most of their hours when they weren't onstage were spent going from bar to bar and getting thoroughly soused. On one occasion, after spending the night carousing through the city, they returned to their hotel, rode up to the tenth floor and hurled a heavy pot of sand through a window. Fortunately, no one was hurt. Another time they ended a similar spree early in the morning by going from door to door of people's homes and helping themselves to bagfuls of freshly delivered rolls. After satisfying their hunger, our playful chorus boys then proceeded to have a fight with the rolls in the street and in the hotel lobby. One more day in Wilmington and we all would have been thrown out.

The show's New York opening—on April 26, 1928—took place at the

Mansfield Theatre. The performance went well and the next day's reviews were mostly raves. Still, at least half a dozen critics couldn't help pointing out the resemblance between *Present Arms* and *Hit the Deck,* which had opened exactly one year before. Perhaps because of this, the show lasted only a little more than four months.

It was during the run of *Present Arms* that I had my first and only brush with a member of New York's underworld. One of the girls in the cast had actually adopted the stage name of Hotsy-Totsy, but before the opening we managed to talk her into using something a bit more conventional, and she settled on Demaris Doré. She had a solo, "Crazy Elbows," which came toward the end of the first act. One night I was standing in the back of the theatre when the drummer made a mistake during her song and Hotsy-Totsy used a one-syllable vulgarity to express her displeasure that was easily audible in the rear of the house. As the audience let out a collective gasp, I rushed backstage and told the stage manager to get rid of her. Louis Shurr, the agent, sent us a cute little kid as replacement, but because her voice was weak we had to turn her down.

The following night Dorothy and I went to see Marilyn Miller in *Rosalie,* the big Ziegfeld hit at the New Amsterdam. While we were standing on the sidewalk during the intermission, Shurr, his face chalk-white, dashed over to us and told me that we were all in great danger. It seems that the girl we had just turned down was a particularly close friend of one of Brooklyn's most notorious gangsters, and he was determined to avenge this slight to his inamorata. According to Shurr, Larry Fay, another gangster and friend of the Brooklyn hood, wanted to see me that very night and would be waiting for me at twelve-thirty at Texas Guinan's speakeasy.

Putting up a brave front, I told Shurr to go home and assured him I could smooth things over. As nonchalantly as possible, Dorothy and I returned to our seats for the second act of *Rosalie,* though neither of us had the foggiest idea of what was going on. Despite my objection, Dorothy insisted on staying with me after the show. Because we were early for the scheduled encounter, we first went to our favorite late-night port of call, Montmartre, until it was time to learn whether my lack of artistic appreciation would condemn me to be taken for a ride or dumped in the river. When we arrived at the appointed hour, Texas Guinan seated us at an isolated table in the corner. Presently she returned with a tall, black-haired, gray-faced man with a sagging jaw who looked like an undertaker—which, in a way, he was. Before saying anything to me, Larry Fay stared at our departing hostess and muttered, "She's a son of a bitch." Even in the dimly lit room I could see Dorothy blush; language like that was simply not used in what was then called mixed company, and it served to make both of us even more apprehensive. Fay then turned to me, reached across the table, squeezed my wrist, and in a voice of gravel, said, "As a special favor to me, Dick, wouldja let the girl go on for one performance?"

When Larry Fay asks for a special favor like that, how could any fearless composer possibly refuse? The next night the girl went on, and she was terrible. As I left the theatre during the intermission, Fay was waiting for me at the curb. Uh-oh, I thought, here it comes. Now he's going to tell me she's another Marilyn Miller and as a special favor to him I'll have to give her the leading part and put her name in lights. Fay looked at me coldly and said, "She stinks, and what's more, I'm gonna tell her so myself." Then he squeezed my wrist again and said pointedly, "Listen, if there's ever anything you want done, just let me know and I'll take care of it for you."

That was the end of the matter and also the end of my association with the underworld. But I must confess that there have been two or three times in my life when I was sorely tempted to avail myself of Fay's generous offer.

One afternoon in the spring of 1928 I was working at the piano at home when suddenly my grandfather appeared in the doorway and said, "Richard, I don't feel well." I got him to his bedroom and phoned down to my father's office on the first floor of the apartment house we lived in. Pop was in our apartment within minutes, and his immediate diagnosis was that surgery was imperative. Grandpa wasn't strong enough to be moved to a hospital, so we had to turn his bedroom into an operating room. But the operation wasn't successful and a week later he died. It hit me terribly hard. I adored the old man, as did my brother and my parents. I knew he had no faith in the theatre as a career, but his hope that I would go into a more conventional line of work was motivated only by his deep concern for what he felt was best for me. When I did achieve a measure of success, he never hesitated to tell me how proud he was of me and of what I'd accomplished.

After Grandpa's death I felt that I had to get away alone for a while, so I took a brief trip to Colorado Springs. While there, I began getting frantic telephone calls from Larry and Herb about a new idea they had for a musical. It was to be based on a novel called *The Son of the Grand Eunuch,* and they were both convinced that it had the makings of a sensational musical. Sensational was right. I bought the book, read it, and thought they were both crazy. The story was about a young man in ancient China who did everything he could to avoid being castrated, a prerequisite for inheriting his father's exalted title. This didn't strike me as a theatrically adaptable subject for the musical stage, but Larry and Herb had already talked Lew Fields into producing it, and I found myself in the uncomfortable position of being the lone holdout.

When I returned to New York, we continued thrashing the matter around until I finally agreed to go along. They were all so sure of themselves that I didn't want to be the one to torpedo a project they all believed in so deeply. One factor that helped influence me was that while I found the story distasteful, I had to admit that it was a daring departure from the average Broadway musical-comedy subject. Maybe we could shock people into liking it. *Present Arms* had turned out to be a fair success, but there was nothing out of the ordinary about its theme and I certainly didn't relish hearing people compare it to *Hit the Deck.* With *Chee-Chee,* which was the name of our castration musical, there surely wouldn't be any danger of its being compared to anything. Furthermore, from a strictly creative standpoint it offered the challenge of introducing an entirely new concept within the framework of musical theatre.

Larry and I had long been firm believers in the close unity of song and story, but we were not always in a position to put our theories into practice. *Chee-Chee* gave us that chance. To avoid the eternal problem of the story coming to a halt as the songs take over, we decided to use a number of short pieces of from four to sixteen bars each, with no more than six songs of traditional form and length in the entire score. In this way the music would be an essential part of the structure of the story rather than an appendage to the action. The concept was so unusual, in fact, that we even called attention to it with the following notice in the program:

> NOTE: The musical numbers, some of them very short, are so interwoven with the story that it would be confusing for the audience to peruse a complete list.

Chee-Chee also brought up a specific problem about the actual writing of the score. With the exception of *Dearest Enemy* and about three quarters of *A Connecticut Yankee,* all our other previous musicals had had modern settings, mostly in or around New York City. For *Chee-Chee,* my job was to compose music for a story set in ancient China. Obviously it would have been inappropriate for me to write typically "American" music, but equally obviously, even if I could have written "Chinese" music, Broadway audiences would have found it unattractive—to say nothing of the impossibility of Larry's finding the proper words to go with it. The only solution was to compose my own kind of music but with an Oriental inflection, reproducing a style rather than creating a faithful imitation. Frequently composers try to reproduce the musical sound of a specific age or locale, often with some success, but I think it's a mistake. It leaves the writer wide open to comparison—usually unfavorable—with the real thing, and at best only reveals re-creative, rather than creative, skills.